Eric Laws

Tourist destination management

Issues, analysis and policies

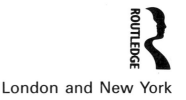

London and New York

First published 1995
by Routledge
11 New Fetter Lane, London EC4P 4EE

Simultaneously published in the USA and Canada
by Routledge
29 West 35th Street, New York, NY 10001

© 1995 Eric Laws

Typeset in Times by Florencetype Ltd, Stoodleigh, Devon
Printed and bound in Great Britain by Biddles Ltd,
Guildford and King's Lynn

British Library Cataloguing in Publication Data
A catalogue record for this book is available from the
British Library

Library of Congress Cataloging in Publication Data
 Laws, Eric, 1945–
  Tourist destination management: issues, analysis and policies /
 Eric Laws.
  p. cm. – (Routledge topics in tourism)
  Includes bibliographical references and index.
  ISBN 0–415–10591–9
  1. Tourist trade. I. Title. II. Series.
 G155.A1L3775 1995
 338.4′79104 – dc20

                                                    94–32453
                                                    CIP

ISBN 0–415–10591–9

1 Week Loan

This book is due for return on or before the last date shown below

Routledge Topics in Tourism

Series Adviser:
Stephen Page, Massey University Albany, Auckland

Routledge Topics in Tourism offers a fresh, concise grounding in key themes in tourism and leisure. Each book in the series acts as a succinct and stimulating introduction to a particular topic and provides:

- comprehensive discussions of concepts
- international case studies
- key point summaries
- short questions for discussion

This series will be an excellent resource for students of tourism and leisure options at undergraduate and diploma levels.

Already published:

Transport for Tourism
Stephen Page, Massey University Albany, Auckland

Forthcoming titles include:

People in Tourism
Tom Baum, University of Buckingham

Tourism Policy
C. Michael Hall, University of Canberra
John Jenkins, University of Central Queensland

Urban Tourism
Stephen Page, Massey University Albany, Auckland

Contents

Figures

Tables

Case study themes

CASE	Pg	Impacts				Stakeholders					Focus		
		Economic	Cultural	Environmental	Ecological	Residents	Investors	Industry	Employees	Tourists	Planning	Synergy	Marketing
Majorca			*	*				*					+
Canterbury			*			*				+	+		
Britain							+			*			
Wales								*		*			
Tonga			*			+							
Manu				*	*				+				
Samoa			*								+		
Tibet		+	+		*				*				
Antarctica				+	*			+					
L'Angleterre Sud								*				+	
Nottingham								*					+
Hawaii						*	*				+		
South Africa		*	+			*	+				*	+	
Dubai		*	*	+	+	+	+	+	+	*	+	*	*

* Major theme + Minor theme

Preface

People go on holiday to enjoy themselves in relatively unfamiliar surroundings, but their activities have important consequences for different groups, representing opportunities for employment and profit, or causing nuisance and disrupting the established patterns of life in destination areas. This divergent view of tourism raises ethical issues concerning the distribution of benefits arising from visitors' activities amongst the various interest groups in a destination, the residents, investors, employees and tourists themselves.

The study of tourist destinations may seem somewhat trivial when set against the social and economic conditions in many South American, African and Asiatic countries which are host to tourists from the wealthy European, American and South East Asian states. Tourists expect to find the familiar high standards of accommodation and hygiene, and countries which wish to attract tourists have to devote financial and physical resources to the construction of airports, hotels, roads and other amenities which have little relevance to the majority of the population. Tourists are attracted by the exotic aspects of destinations, and facilities are built in remote locations so that they can photograph rare animals or watch villagers perform traditional dances. Despite its hedonistic aspects, and the privileged nature of tourists themselves, the significance of tourism has been recognised at the highest political levels in many countries with serious, even urgent economic and social needs. In March 1994, Peter Mokaba, Chairman of the African National Congress (ANC) Tourism Forum, discussed the

importance which would be accorded to tourism in the new South
Africa following the first free elections on 28 April of that year.
The following remarks are drawn from the views he put forward at a
seminar for British tourism managers.

> The ANC's objective is to achieve 'one people in a united non-racial,
> non-sexist and democratic society and country', and tourism has an
> instrumental role to play in our seeking to realise this destiny.
>
> High on the agenda of people's expectations of their new free-
> dom is their physical needs. Providing houses for people who can
> neither buy, rent nor maintain them does satisfy a need, but only
> in the short term. It is a material oriented approach to develop-
> ment which shows little interest in the person. It leaves people
> without the means to maintain and manage development in a
> way which would guarantee forward movement. Employment,
> which produces the income to satisfy these needs, is the pressing
> demand. People need to earn sufficient money not only to satisfy
> their physical needs, but also their needs of security and social
> esteem.
>
> Of the industries necessary to stimulate and develop the economy,
> South African tourism is of high economic significance. It could make
> a vital contribution to sustained economic growth in South Africa.
> Yet, despite the country's unique attractions of wildlife and game
> parks, dramatic scenic beauty, superb climate and great cultural
> riches, South Africa has failed to capture its share of the world
> market, it has less than a quarter of one per cent of world tourist
> arrivals.
>
> Tourism is a bridge builder of understanding amongst people and
> an effective mechanism of cultural exchange. Communities will thus
> not only benefit materially, but also spiritually through active and
> increased tourism. In addition, tourists often seek to purchase
> cultural artefacts, and this enhances the local community's economic
> gains.
>
> Through its message of goodwill and hospitality, tourism could
> act as a key nation builder, reversing the arrested development of
> South Africa as a nation, creating bonds between South Africans
> and other people of the world through interaction, exchange and edu-
> cation.
>
> Through its rich endowment of natural heritage, cultural diversity,
> infrastructure and climate, South Africa is ideally positioned to take

advantage of an awakening interest in its peoples, its places and its mysteries.

Further discussion of the development of tourism in South Africa can be found in Chapter 5.

Eric Laws
Napier University, Edinburgh
1995

Acknowledgements

Books which examine issues and policies in a human activity as diverse as tourism cannot be prepared in isolation, although the process of writing them is a solitary task. Many people have influenced this book, both directly by contributing to the case studies, and indirectly through helping the author to develop his own understanding of tourism. Most of the case studies in this book are based on detailed discussions with the managers responsible for particular destinations, and I wish to express my gratitude for their time and insights, and for access to specialised consultancy reports. The views expressed here, although derived from the many sources cited in the text, are my own, and I accept responsibility for any errors in the text.

Three other groups of people deserve recognition. The authors of many tourism, marketing and management books have influenced my own writing; the colleagues and students with whom I have discussed much of this book have provided constructive comments, and the experts who speak at meetings of the Tourism Society and the Chartered Institute of Marketing Travel Industry Group have contributed significantly to my understanding. To all of these, and to my travelling companion, I extend my thanks.

While every effort has been made to contact the copyright holders of all material which is quoted in this book, there may be some who have been missed. The author and publishers ask that any such sources contact Routledge direct.

Eric Laws
Napier University, Edinburgh
1995

Introduction

As tourism activity increases in scale and variety, it becomes increasingly important to understand its effects on the places which people visit for their leisure. This book examines the main issues and discusses examples of current management practice around the world, applying modern theories to the analysis of how destinations develop and compete. It considers the ways they attempt to reconcile tasks which sometimes conflict. They are trying to attract visitors and investors to an area, and having done so, they must satisfy not only them but the residents, as well as improving the local environment and protecting the ecology of the area.

Virtually every human settlement has a long tradition of visits by traders and missionaries, but a place can only become a destination for modern tourism as a result of two sets of related activities. These are the local development of facilities which cater to the needs of tourists, and marketing efforts carried out in the areas from which tourists originate.

With no formal tourism development, a remote Pacific island may be visited only by islanders working overseas who return to visit relatives, and by occasional yachtsmen, but until it has an international airport, several hotels, many restaurants and a wide range of interesting activities for temporary visitors, it cannot compete in the brochures of tour operators, and is not a destination which can serve the modern industry of tour operators. To become as successful a destination as Hawaii, visited by more than six million people in 1993, an island requires more than exotic scenery, a mild tropical climate, beaches and reefs, and a friendly, welcoming ambience. Decisions had to be taken about how to develop the islands' infrastructure and tourism facilities, investment had to be procured, staff had to be recruited and trained. Further decisions were required about how to publicise Hawaii's attractions, images had to be created which best conveyed their particular characteristics to potential visitors of the type the islands' tourism managers wished to attract.

The contexts for decisions such as these are the developments being carried out by competing destinations, and the importance accorded to tourism against other priorities in the development of a destination's infrastructure, economy and society. Tourists' activities have consequences not only for the staff and managers they come into contact with, but also for the residents, environment and ecology of destination areas. Therefore, tourism development proposals ought to be evaluated in terms of the change they are likely to cause to all the elements of that area.

Accepting delivery of the first 747 in 1959, the wide-bodied jet which Pan Am had been instrumental in commissioning from the Boeing Company, Juan Tripp, Pan Am's founder and Chairman, spoke of the potential impact of international tourism as being more powerful than the atom bomb. Since then, the equivalent of a quarter of the world's population has travelled abroad and the consequences can be seen in the development of airports, hotels and resorts in most countries of the world.

The effects of tourism on particular regions such as the Alps or the Mediterranean have been well documented. Villages, valleys, forests, pasture land and peaks have come under pressure from increasing tourism developments such as ski runs. In the Alps the results include deforestation, landslides and avalanches, overcrowding and noise pollution. Along much of the Mediterranean coast, remote fishing villages have been transformed into tourist resorts with a completely different pace of life, and romantic, isolated archeological and historical sites are daily visited by so many people that they appear to be located in coach parks. These factors will be examined in subsequent chapters, but two issues can immediately be noted:

● Tourism brings changes which have serious consequences for residents in destination areas.

- Destination areas (which are often dependent on tourism for income and employment) face the risk of damage to their tourist appeal from the success of the industry itself, as it brings increasing numbers of visitors.

Similarly, man-made environments also come under pressure from tourism development. Local politicians and newspapers complain that great buildings including the Parthenon and Notre Dame are being eroded by the constant pressure of visitors' feet. Condensation and dust resulting from the large numbers of visitors have damaged the painted ceiling of the Sistine Chapel, and although this has been restored and remains open to tourists, they have been excluded from many other sites including the prehistoric cave paintings in the Dordogne, and from Tutankhamen's tomb in an attempt to halt their rapid, and very recent, deterioration.

The positive side of the tourism industry is well documented. Tourists' spending can enhance an area by bringing wealth and stimulating employment, enterprise and infrastructure development. The interest which drew tourists to a particular area can encourage the preservation of its unique features of local heritage and culture, and give a rationale for the protection of natural environments or the ecology of the area while providing a source of finance to improve access to them for visitors and residents alike.

The challenge to countries in an era of global travel and investment is to retain their own identity, yet absorb modernism. Tourism produces pressures on destinations to conform to internationally-accepted standards of accommodation and food hygiene, and to be tolerant of visitors' relatively unstructured vacation behaviour. For the tourist, the experience of travel can enhance individual understanding of different countries and cultures, or reaffirm the tourist's own identity through superficial encounters which reinforce his or her stereotypes of foreigners and foreign places. The predominant form of the tourism industry is organised group tours and this re-inforces this potential for confrontational meetings with foreigners, showing people selected and often artificial aspects of destinations' culture.

One of the most optimistic signs at the end of the twentieth century is the emerging consensus that although the world's ability to sustain all forms of life is not infinite, improved technology has demonstrated ways of managing existing resources more efficiently, so that renewal and use are becoming twin aspects of policy. Husbandry of natural resources is not a new concept to society, coppicing represents a way of cropping woodland which was well understood by medieval Europeans, and similarly most settled communities have developed ways to exploit the local flora, fauna and mineral resources without prejudicing its ability to renew itself. However, modern technology has also led to a vast increase in the human population of the planet, and other technical advances have improved our ability to move around it, thus bringing a new form of pressure, tourism, to regions which have often very frail environments.

Managed sensitively, tourism can be less destructive than alternative industries such as mining, while it has the potential to increase the wealth of the population in destination areas, thus making communities more viable and providing a clear justification for devoting resources to the preservation of local culture, heritage and environmental features.

In its mass forms, tourism is a very recent phenomenon, and until recently, most destination development was carried out on a speculative or *ad hoc* basis. Although 1,619 different plans were identified in a 1980 study by the World Tourist Organisation (WTO), Gunn (1988b) reports that few had considered the socio-economic impacts likely to result, nor had they taken into consideration the competition from alternative destinations. Gunn advocated a planning approach to tourism and leisure project development, but this raises a number of other questions of concern to all with a stake in destination management.

- Who decides on the nature, scale and speed of development for tourism?
- To what extent are the concerns of the various groups involved, such as visitors, residents, investors and employees recognised and responded to?

Destinations are highly varied, and each faces a unique set of problems and opportunities. Consequently, it is rather difficult to make generalised statements about tourist destinations which are universally applicable: it is precisely the differences between places, and the individuality of visitors, residents and the natural environment and ecology of each destination which makes tourism both an exciting human activity and a fascinating field of study. Two methodologies to counter this diversity have been adopted in this book.

1 The systems model introduced in Chapter 1 enables a variety of analytical approaches drawn from sociology, economics and other fields of study to be applied to any destination, highlighting the critical aspects of each.

2 The book provides readers with a number of case studies illustrating particular points, for example the planning approach recommended by WTO for Samoa, the concerns about further resort development voiced by Hawaii's residents and government, and the opportunities which tourism presents to South Africa's first freely elected government.

The cases have the pedagogical advantage of showing that the issues in destination management, although they can be isolated for analysis, must be considered in the wider, systemic perspective of a functioning economy, society and ecology. The table of contents indicates the main and subsidiary themes of each of these case studies.

It is hoped that these short case studies will prove interesting to independent readers, while being particularly useful as a basis for group discussions, role play and similar participative learning and teaching strategies for students on taught courses. Each case concludes by posing one question, although lecturers may wish to suggest alternative exercises in the light of their own teaching style and syllabus.

Each chapter is also followed by a series of exercises inviting readers to consider some of the methods and issues in the context of destinations familiar to them. A list of relevant books is also given after each chapter – these were selected either because they extend aspects of the argument introduced in the chapter, or because they present additional, or alternative perspectives and approaches. Reading these books, and pursuing some of the references contained in the bibliography, will deepen readers' understanding of the complex range of issues which are introduced in this book.

The first chapter will review the key issues and introduce the general systems model as a basis for the analysis of destination management issues and policies. Chapter 2 will examine the factors in tourists' choice of destination to visit, and influencing their satisfaction during a stay. Chapter 3 is concerned with the impacts of tourists' activities on the destination's culture, economy, environment and ecology. Chapter 4 introduces readers to the marketing of tourist destinations, focusing attention on the selection of appropriate images and discussing the relative marketplace strengths of destinations and other organisations such as tour operators which influence the extent and type of tourist activity. Policy and planning for tourist destination development is the subject of Chapter 5, which also distinguishes the varying roles and influence of investors, developers, politicians, experts and residents. Chapter 6 discusses the importance given to tourism development and management in Dubai, where Western technologies and finance are welcomed and where leisure and tourism is encouraged within its Islamic traditions.

1
Issues in analysing and managing tourist destinations

Introduction

The success of a tourist destination depends on the regular arrival of large numbers of visitors, and the effects of their activities while they stay there. The flow of tourists to a destination is determined by several factors, including the destination's accessibility, the relative expense of visits, and how aware potential visitors are of the attractions and amenities it offers. As it becomes more successful, a destination undergoes a series of changes resulting from the new business opportunities which tourist spending creates, the need for expanded and improved infrastructure, and the impacts of visitors on the area's culture, economy, environment and ecology.

The modern form of tourism, with large numbers of people regularly travelling far away from home for short, intense periods of leisure is very recent, and while the popularity of exotic long-haul destinations has increased, previously successful destinations such as Britain's many seaside resorts have declined. They had prospered until air-transport-based packaged holidays tempted tourists to the Mediterranean, the Alps and further afield where the climate, scenery, way of life and standards of tourist facilities were enticingly different (Soane, 1993). Over a period of time, tourists' preferences for particular destinations and activities will probably change again, under the influence of several factors, some attracting clients to 'new' destinations, others acting as repellents! The former category includes further improvements in access resulting from infrastructure development, particularly new regional airports, or more regular air links. Examples of factors inhibiting tourism development are civil unrest, inflation, or natural events such as earthquakes, huge forest fires or outbreaks of disease. A third category influencing choice of destination is policy decisions by investors or politicians regarding tourism. Major hotel companies have developed large, high quality resorts in previously isolated regions. Religious fundamentalism has resulted in the virtual closure of countries such as Iran to Western tourists, while other countries such as China have encouraged the development of a tourism sector for the economic and social benefits expected.

The dynamics of destination development

Figure 1.1 illustrates the phases of destination development. As tourist activity stimulates investment in hotels, amenities and infrastructure, the expanding resort therefore becomes more reliant on arrivals, and undertakes promotional campaigns to attract additional tourists. However, the cycle of destination development also includes downturns in tourism as a consequence of interruptions caused by a variety of factors such as a natural catastrophe, or the development of newer, more attractive destinations elsewhere. These interruptions jeopardise the flow of revenue which is required to sustain investment programmes required to keep a destination competitive with others.

There is an important distinction to be drawn between the arrival in an area of occasional, individual travellers and its later management both as a destination for large numbers of tourists and as the centre for its resident community. In the 'pre-tourism phase', the main reason for visiting an area is to see friends and relatives, or for business. Such visitors generally take an active interest in the natural and cultural features which they are taken to see, and their requirements for catering, accommodation and entertainment are easily absorbed by the facilities supporting the local community: in effect they become a temporary part of the community. At this early stage of destination development few businesses are dependent on visitors for their trade.

Under the pressure of increasing arrivals as mass tourism develops, the business sector responds with the development of specialised services for visitors and so the area begins to take on the familiar characteristics of a tourist destination. Restaurants and bars are opened, catering specifically for visitors with dishes which are familiar to them,

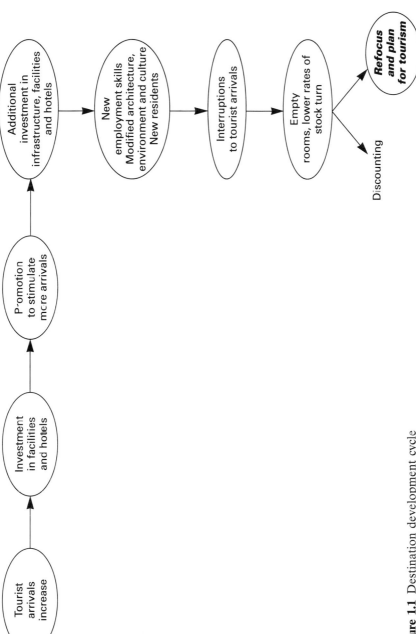

Figure 1.1 Destination development cycle

shops display and sell souvenirs, many of which are imported. New skills and accompanying attitudes to technology, work practices and towards visitors are sought by employers investing in the tourism sector. The relatively high remuneration offered by the tourism sector in some countries reinforces these changing values, and may reduce the attractiveness of traditional employment. Overall, the economy of the destination is likely to shift in response to the profit opportunities offered by mass tourism, and a variety of legitimate and some rather questionable ways of serving the financially important population of temporary visitors will emerge.

While the expectations of visitors increasingly drive local entre-preneurs' decisions, members of the resident community also begin to emulate aspects of their visitors' behaviour. Cumulatively, the effect is to induce and support an increasing acceptance of changes in the character and nature of the destination's social, moral and personal relationships. Traditional styles of eating, dress codes, working patterns, and social and personal relationships change as the resort develops. The changes result in the 'tourism management phase', which is charac-terised by two approaches:

1 The need to market the destination in order to attract sufficient visitors to sustain its tourism business activities.
2 The adoption of administrative methods to ensure beneficial forms of tourism.

During the tourism management phase, destination authorities begin to take proactive decisions about what facilities to offer, trying to anticipate the demands and changing tastes of their visitors, and attempting to influence the nature of their experiences. The local government authorities also have to cope with an expanding and changing resident population as experienced managers with their families, and young employees are attracted by new work opportun-ities. The arrival of new residents to service the destination's tourists further distorts the original relationship between tourists and the community, and may lead to friction as the incomers are often thought to displace local people in the lucrative and exciting tourism sector of the labour market. This seems more likely to occur when local communities are resistant to the requirements of the new modes of shift working in the service sector of the economy. Further-more, it is the new residents who are most likely to become guides for visitors, and act as interpreters of local history and culture, even though they do not share the traditions, tastes and values of the original inhabitants.

The changing nature of a destination under these influences means that it will appeal to different types of visitor at different phases of its development. Some resorts have seen their clientele change completely over a relatively short period of time. The Côte d'Azur was originally known as a winter resort, although now it is busiest in the summer, and while it used to cater almost exclusively to the rich, it now serves tourists representing a cross-section of Western European society, excluding only the poorest sectors. Case study A examines some of the factors influencing recent improvements in Majorca.

While the occasional pre-tourism traveller visiting an area was generally regarded as an honoured guest in the community, modern mass tourism is an industry built on the sale and purchase of hospitality.

> The most noticeable impact of tourism on traditional values is that certain social and human relations are brought into the economic sphere: they become part of making a living . . . goods or services that used to be part of peoples social lives have now been commercialised and are offered as commodities.
>
> (De Kadt, 1979)

In developing countries, tourism is often regarded as a potent 'modernising' influence on values and morals. Some governments see these effects as beneficial, and their policy decisions encourage the tourism in all areas of the country. In other cultural contexts modern isation is regarded as a cause for concern, and ways are sought to limit the transfer of new values from tourists to the local community. MacCannell (1976) has commented on one extreme form of development, which he referred to as plantation tourism. 'Tourism may be regarded as a new kind of industry building factories called resorts and amusement parks. . . . Some come close to imprisoning tourists within resort compounds.' MacCannell pointed out that this type of plantation tourism is exploitative on both sides; tourists have minimal contact with local people, and locals do not benefit from the money that tourism generates because it is retained by the resort's owners, and they are often based in the tourists' countries of origin.

Case study A

Destination improvements in Majorca

Majorca was one of the first destinations for mass tourism in the Mediterranean, but visitor numbers began to fall at the end of the 1980s, suggesting that it was losing its appeal due to over-familiarity, falling standards relative to alternative Eastern Mediterranean or long-haul destinations, and adverse publicity in its main origin markets featuring the unruly behaviour of some visitors.

Majorca's problems were exacerbated since 90 per cent of its visitors were clients of charter-based inclusive tour operators (WTO, 1979), bringing high-volume low-yield business. Furthermore, pressure during the 1970s and 1980s from the large overseas tour operators had forced hotel rates down, and although this strategy succeeded in attracting large numbers of visitors, the low room rates meant that hotels could not afford to modernise or refurbish their facilities in line with competing destinations. The situation was further worsened since another response to the increased arrivals through the 1980s had been the building of low-grade hotel stock, and as a result Majorca gained a reputation for building activity, blocked views, and the spreading of hotels to previously unspoiled areas. These difficulties of environmental deterioration were compounded by frequent, and highly publicised flight delays from Northern Europe across French airspace, and the tour operators' tendency to alter clients' accommodation arrangements on arrival.

Co-ordinated approaches were adopted to improve visitors' experiences and to obtain increased financial benefit from each visitor.

- From 1985 onwards, development controls limited building permits to four-star or better properties, with a maximum height of three storeys, and required 30 square metres of land per guest.
- In Magaluff, measures to improve the quality of the environment included tree planting, pedestrianisation, and a public sea front esplanade to replace privately owned hotel and café frontages.

Case study A *(continued)*

- A wider customer mix was sought by attracting tour operators from The Netherlands and Switzerland, and by inviting quality press visits to other aspects of Majorca, drawing attention away from the established resort areas near Palma in favour of the modern, architecturally more sensitive resorts on the East coast.
- Overseas youth tour operators co-operated by repositioning their services as well organised and behaved. Large same-sex groups were prohibited, and representatives roles were redefined, they no longer lead drinking competitions!
- Thomsons embarked on a programme to invest £10 million in ten three-star properties. Detailed specifications were prepared covering food, facilities, entertainment, room decor, and service standards expected from staff.

The improvements to Majorca's tourism standards should be seen in the context of the Spanish government's four-year improvement plan (1991–95) for tourism, focusing on the appropriate development of the industry in the light of Spain's heritage and other resources (Jenner and Smith, 1993). The intention is to improve the product rather than expand capacity.

Sources: based on Morgan (1991), articles in *Travel News*, March 1990 and the *Travel Trade Gazette*, May 1990, and interviews with tourism managers.

Suggested exercise

For any holiday resort with which you are familiar, identify the key problems for residents and visitors, and recommend appropriate improvements.

The elements of tourist destinations

Two factors contribute to the attractiveness of a tourism region. The *primary* features include its climate, ecology, cultural traditions, traditional architecture and its land forms. *Secondary* destination features are the developments introduced specifically for tourists, such as hotels, catering, transport, activities and amusements.

The distinction between primary and secondary tourism resources draws attention to a striking characteristic of many tourist destinations. Tourists are often able to enjoy a destination's primary resources, for example, the beach, a cathedral, or the ambience of a well-preserved Georgian city without directly paying for any of these facilities (although there are costs associated with maintaining each of them). However, the development of an area's tourism industry is dependent on the secondary facilities available in the region, and these are invariably priced because they are provided by commercial organisations.

Any tourist destination can be distinguished from others by research to identify the variety, quality and range of activities and amenities it provides for visitors. Three steps are required.

First, the researcher decides on relevant elements to examine, such as beaches, accommodation and restaurants. Museums, speciality retailers, car rental businesses and many others are relevant in particular destinations.

Second, an audit is conducted for each category of tourism facility to determine the number and quality of resources available, identifying their capacity, opening hours, accessibility to disabled or elderly users, and their pricing policy.

The first two steps in the procedure can be carried out by observation at the destination, or by desk research based on the analysis of brochures and directories, and provides the researcher with a detailed understanding of the range and extent of a destination's tourist resources. The third step identifies how visitors themselves make use of the destination's resources.

Third, a survey is conducted to determine the number (or proportion) of tourists in particular categories using each type of facility. As Figure 1.2 shows, by distinguishing the different behaviour of important categories of visitor, an understanding of their particular interests and needs can be reached as a basis for future development, or for marketing programmes.

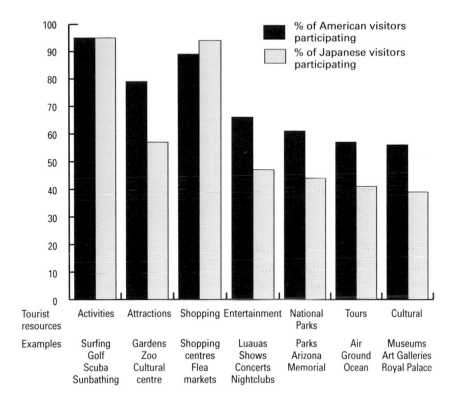

Figure 1.2 The range and use of Hawaii's tourist resources
Based on: Hawaii Visitor Bureau, 1991.

A way of conceptualising the complexity of tourism products has been proposed by Middleton (1988), which he called the total tourism product (TTP). The components of the TTP can be classified under headings which include the natural and man-made attractions of an area, its facilities and services, the ease of access to it and the images which are used to attract tourists to it. The final element in the TTP is the total cost of the holiday. These approaches are useful in emphasising to managers the interdependence of the many elements in destination systems which together form the basis of tourists' experiences.

Patterns of tourist activity

An understanding of the factors which determine tourist activity is fundamental to destination management and the analysis of tourist destinations, Table 1.1 summarises the key points which stimulate flows between the places from which tourists originate, and their destinations.

Table 1.1 Factors stimulating tourist flows between an origin and a destination

*	Easy access
*	Affordability
*	Ethnic or historic links
*	Interesting activities, scenery, culture and climate
*	Familiarity *or* exoticness
*	Marketing effort

The factors which link an origin and a destination must also be considered in the wider context of streams of tourists crossing the globe; the World Tourist Organization (WTO) recorded 476 million tourist arrivals in 1992, of which 60 per cent were in Europe. Two perspectives are discussed in the following sections:

1 Spatial analysis of the factors linking origins and destinations.
2 Temporal analysis, to examine the seasonal factors in tourism.

Spatial aspects of global tourist activity

The patterns of tourist movement between different areas of the world reflect the culture, climate, economy and stage of development of the areas where tourists normally live, and of the places they visit. Three spatial patterns are considered here.

Cross-border tourism

Many countries which share common borders, such as the USA with Canada or Mexico, or close neighbours like Britain and France, are linked by strong flows of visitors. Their differing cultures, combined with their proximity to each other provides a rationale for business trips and short breaks or longer leisure visits. The phenomenon is enhanced by price differentials when the same goods are bought in different countries (reflecting differing VAT rates or the availability of 'duty free' shopping privileges for travellers between them). Other factors attracting tourist flows in specific directions are different restrictions on activities such as gambling, prostitution or drinking.

Flows to the tourism periphery

The second tourist stream is a complex set of links between the wealthier population centres of the world and varied destinations which are distant from where they live. One example characterising this type of flow is variously described as from the 'frost belt to the sun belt' or from 'smoke stack to blue sky', for example from the northern American States and Canada to Florida, the Caribbean or Hawaii, and from Scandinavia, Britain, and Germany (amongst others) to the Mediterranean resorts, the Canary Islands, or to an increasing range of long-haul destinations. Such is the significance of this type of tourism that Turner and Ash entitled their 1975 study, *The Golden Hordes, International Tourism and the Pleasure Periphery*. Similarly, in the winter many tourists from urban and industrial centres travel to skiing resorts in the Rocky Mountains, or the Alps.

The core regions from which most tourists originate are characterised by a high population density, well-developed infrastructure and a dynamic society and economy. Tourists' destinations are often 'peripheral' areas, typified by exotic, less economically privileged regions, such as Turkey, Bali, Kenya or China. As Page (1992) has pointed out 'various countries on the periphery (of the EC) have benefited from a growing internationalisation of tourism and the search for new tourist destinations'.

The appeal of peripheral areas lies in their natural or cultural differences from familiar conditions in tourists' origin areas. Generally, peripheral areas are less developed economically, and in consequence work may be scarce and labour is likely to be cheap. Since tourism is an intensive employment industry, its development in these areas offers advantages to the local community. While visitors benefit from lower prices resulting from lower costs, their presence generates jobs. On the other hand, elements of any peripheral destination such as its ecology or cultural traditions may be susceptible to damage from tourism activity, in part because there is a lower experience of adapting to external pressures for change than in the developed core areas from which the visitors come, and also because these areas often lack legislative and planning controls to protect against inappropriate development.

Seasonality in tourism flows

A major characteristic of the tourism industry is the seasonal nature of demand. In some cases the pull of a destination's tourist resources (particularly climate, or sports dependent on climate) largely determines the timing of arrivals, and this primary feature may also account for much of the distribution of tourist activity around the area. The seasonal nature of beach holidays or of skiing, and the specific location of ski resorts in relation to natural features and purpose-built facilities are easy to explain in these terms. In other destinations arrival patterns are determined mainly by driving factors in the originating region, particularly its climate, or socially determined events such as school holiday dates.

Strong seasonality such as is illustrated in Figure 1.3 causes difficulties for destination managers as sufficient facilities to meet peak demand have to be installed and staffed, but at other times of the year the reduced visitor activity cannot sustain the peak level of businesses. Traditional British seaside guest houses used to close entirely for several months in the winter. This seasonal feature of the business was attractive to many semi-retired and amateur owners who themselves wished to take lengthy holidays after the peak season. However, the long-term viability of seasonal destinations is jeopardised, because they are unlikely to generate sufficient cash flow to invest in improvements to their facilities from season to season, and eventually they risk losing business to more adaptable destinations. Shaw and Williams (1987) found that 60 per cent of hotels and guest houses in Looe, Cornwall, had been acquired by new owners between 1984 and 1985, and personal savings were the main source of capital. The authors queried the commitment of proprietors given their high degree of mobility, and suggested that they were attracted to the area by its environmental features, they were unlikely to be enthusiastic about efforts to extend the destination's season.

Uneven flows of business can, however, be influenced by destination marketing programmes designed to stimulate out of season visits, either through pricing tactics or by developing a range of additional activities at off-peak times of the year. Changing tastes and interests can be harnessed too, mountain areas have been able to capitalise on the growing participation in snow sports to develop strong winter business in addition to the summer visitors who are attracted by Alpine scenery and traditions. Another strategy to counter seasonality is to

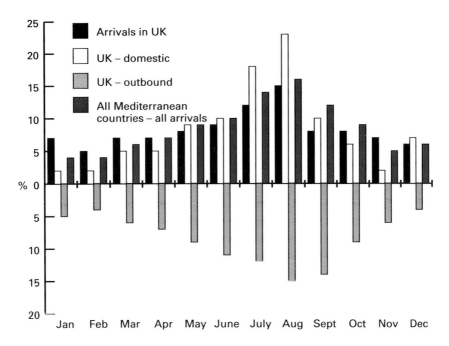

Figure 1.3 Seasonality in tourist flows

Sources: British Home Tourism Survey, International Passenger Survey and Jenner and Smith (1993).

develop links with origins where different factors determine the timing of demand for outbound holidays, to coincide with slack periods in a destination's established pattern of business.

British holiday-taking behaviour

Many visitors are attracted to the great cultural and commercial centres of the world. For example, 18.5 million international visitors arrived in Britain in 1992, attracted by its business opportunities, its great museums and art collections and theatres, as well as the shopping, its countryside and because they were visiting friends or relatives who live there. The scale and complexity of these movements can be seen in Table 1.2, which also indicates the significance of the UK's outbound tourist flows for destination countries, and the value and volume of domestic tourist activity.

The propensity to take holidays, and preferences for destinations changes over time. In Britain, 'the proportion of adults taking a holiday

Table 1.2 Tourist flows to and from Britain

Tourists from Britain			Tourists to Britain		
Rank	Destination	Millions 1992	Millions	Visitors origin	Rank
1	France	7.9	2.7	USA	1
2	Spain	5.7	2.5	France	2
3	USA	2.5	2.3	Germany	3
4	Irish Republic	2.1	1.4	Irish Republic	4
5	Greece	1.9	1.0	The Netherlands	5
6	Germany	1.8	0.8	Italy	6
7	The Netherlands	1.4	0.7	Spain	7
8	Portugal	1.2	0.6	Canada	8
9	Italy	1.2	0.6	Japan	9
10	Gibralta, Malta			Belgium and	
	and Cyprus	1.3	0.8	Luxembourg	10

Total overseas trips: 33.8 million   Total visitors from overseas: 18.5 million
Total spending on   Total overseas visitors'
   overseas trips: £11 billion   spending: £8 billion

               Total domestic holidays: 95.6 million
               Total spending on
                  domestic holidays: £10.7 billion

Source: Cooper and Latham (1994).

in 1992 was the same as 25 years ago, but 24 per cent take two or more holidays (up from 7 per cent in 1966)' (CSO, 1994). Until 1970, only 34 per cent of the British population had ever taken an overseas holiday, but within a decade the proportion had increased to 56 per cent, and by 1990, 70 per cent of Britons had been abroad. The popularity of holidays, and the importance of decisions about the next to be taken can be gauged from the viewing figures for programmes such as *Wish You Were Here* (ITV, Mondays). According to the British Advertising Bureau's figures, over 11 million people regularly watched this feature in early 1994. Its popularity was exceeded only by programmes such as *Coronation Street*, *This is Your Life*, *The Bill* and *Emmerdale*!

This rapid increase in overseas holiday taking is not unique to Britain, and people's experience of international destinations suggests that holiday takers are becoming more experienced and knowledgeable as consumers. Holiday takers' increasing sophistication represents an important dynamic in the market place for holidays, as demand for more varied and interesting holidays has stimulated a great diversity of destination choices. Every year tourists are offered more destinations, and more choice of accommodation. The range of available activities increases too, and tours are designed for quite specific interests, for example, bird watching, golf, the performing arts, participating in cooking or craft classes, or living *en famille* in new environments. At the same time, consumer demand has resulted in a tendency for destinations to become rather similar.

> The modern architecture and the multi-national logos of the hotels promise an enclave of familiarity and security. . . . Around the hotels, smaller businesses, often run by expatriates offer a similar reassurance in the form of British, American or German style bars, cafes and supermarkets.
>
> (Morgan, 1994)

Influences on tourism flows

The direction, frequency and intensity of tourist flows are the outcome of several influences, shown in Figure 1.4. The amount of free time and disposable income of residents in tourist origin areas determines the overall volume of demand for travel from that area, *pushing* tourists towards destinations, while the differences in climate, culture and other attractions of the destination *pull* visitors towards it. Over a period of time, the flow linking one destination and one origin stabilises, through familiarity and the institutions of tourism marketing and tour operating. But three groups of factors can disrupt the established flow, with potentially severe consequences for the destination, unless it is able to develop substitute markets from which tourists originate.

1 Events in the country of origin, such as an economic depression, or adverse foreign exchange rates may *inhibit* the outflow of tourists to all destinations.
2 The destination may experience a natural catastrophe or civil unrest, thus *repelling* incoming tourists from all countries of origin, or the government may impose visa requirements for particular types of visitor, or those from particular countries which are not viewed favourably for ideological reasons.
3 Another disruption to established travel patterns is the development of new destinations (or setting their prices at more accessible levels). This has the effect of *diverting* existing tourist flows.

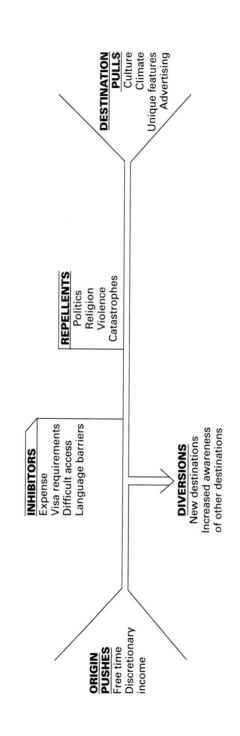

Figure 1.4 Influences on tourist flows

The tourism industry is dependent on peace, and major conflicts have worldwide consequences, significantly reducing the demand for all forms of international travel. As a result of the Gulf War crisis in 1991, average load factors on all international airlines fell to about 55 per cent, compared to 66 per cent the previous year. It was more than a year before international business and leisure traffic recovered.

Concepts of tourist destinations

There is a lack of agreement on the meaning of basic terms to describe tourism such as 'destination' or 'resort', and this has to be regarded as a weakness in tourism analysis. The two terms are sometimes used interchangeably, both have been applied to extensive areas, and also to quite localised developments. 'Resort' can mean an established town which has a significant range of tourist facilities (NEDO/Tourism Society, 1992a) or a region within which several holiday centres are

Table 1.3 Typology of tourist destinations

---

1 CAPITAL CITIES

Example: Athens

Major cities attract visitors for tourism, business, family, cultural and administrative reasons. Tourists tend to cluster in particular zones where archaeological, shopping, cultural or entertainment facilities predominate.

2 A DEVELOPED TRADITIONAL CENTRE

Example: Kusadası, Turkey

Long established village retained as the focus for tourism developments. Hotels, bars and other tourist amenities surround the core, either located in a planned pattern or built speculatively. Tourist structures now dominate the area.

2B TOURING CENTRES

Example: Salzburg

A town with a high concentration of secondary tourist facilities, and good transport links both to countries of tourist origin and to the surrounding scenic or cultural attractions.

3 PURPOSE BUILT RESORTS

Example: Disneyland Paris

All infrastructure and amenities are sharply focused on the business of catering to tourists' needs. Buildings date from the same era, and although the architectural style is highly controlled, it may be out of character with the surrounding area. The resort provides all facilities needed by its clients during their stay.

---

located (Inskeep and Kallenbergher, 1992). Individual hotels sometimes promote themselves as self-contained resorts, particularly in America. Gunn (1988) has defined resorts as 'complexes providing a variety of recreations and social settings at one location'.

A preliminary distinction can now be drawn between the different areas which tourists visit. Tourists' destinations range from purpose-built resorts where all the functions are focused on the dominant activity, to capital cities and entire countries where tourism is a minor, if important feature. Table 1.3 introduces a typology which distinguishes between the main types of destination for international tourists, although it should be noted that Pearce (1989) has drawn attention to Wong's work in Malaysia, emphasising the importance of domestic tourists, and their different destination expectations and behaviour.

Tourism is a rapidly developing sphere of human activity, reflecting the changing economic and social conditions which underlie modern views of individual freedom of expression through consumer choice, and the new technologies of transport and data communications which make it possible for large numbers of people to spend their leisure in distant places. As a consequence, destinations have experienced dynamic and rapid changes. The understanding of destinations is also evolving, and their managers are focusing on more fundamental concerns, as Table 1.4 indicates.

Traditionally, governments have emphasised the economic benefits of tourism, such as its ability to generate foreign exchange earnings, taxation revenue, job creation and regional development, but their scope of interest is now widening to include a vision for the future of tourism in the community (Akehurst et al., 1994). Typically, this entails setting limits to its growth or specifying preferred forms of tourist activity which, it is hoped, will minimise the negative consequences that can result from large numbers of temporary visitors. In some situations, as the discussion of South Africa in the Preface and in Chapter 5 shows, the government's vision of tourism's roles also encompasses its potential contribution to social harmony and international recognition.

Tourist destinations are usually identified and resourced in terms of existing administrative boundaries which have their rationale in ancient land-holding patterns, the underlying geology of the area or accidents of political history, rather than in modern perceptions and use of the area by tourists. Increasingly though, co-operative ventures between neighbouring cities, regions or countries are aimed to encourage

Table 1.4 The evolving concept of tourist destinations

---

1   Traditional concepts

'A place where people spend their holidays'

Elements

Place
The structure and evolution of tourism regions
People
Demographics, motivation, participation rates of tourists and destination service employees
Holiday
Tourists' vacation activities

2   Recent concepts

2a 'An area where people choose to spend their holidays, and the effects of their activities'

Elements

Area
Seaside, city, wilderness, remote tribal region . . .
Choice
Individual motivations, holiday companions, alternative places and activities, marketing to influence choice
Effects
Economic, social, environmental and ecological

2b 'Managing the demand for tourism, and managing its effects on the destination'

Elements

Managing demand
Access, quality control, adding benefits, imagery
Managing tourism effects
Setting objectives for tourism, impact and capacity analysis, planning, zoning

3   Emerging concepts of destinations

Elements

* Recognition of plural interests
* Community debate on the role and scale of tourism
* Co-ordination of public and private sector provision
* Managing tourist demand levels
* Influencing tourists' destination behaviour
* Delivering quality destination experiences
* Co-operative regional promotion and development
* The development of tourism theory
* The development of policies for tourist destination management

---

travellers to adopt a regional or international perspective in their itineraries. Often these trace a theme common to the partners such as 'Cathedrals' or 'The Wine Route' through an extensive area, providing tourists with a logical link which supersedes administrative boundaries, builds on common themes even though these are offered by 'competing' attractions. Each makes the others stronger than any one would be alone, thus gaining the advantage of synergy.

The corollary of the expanding supply of tourism services throughout the world is increased competition between destinations for visitors and their spending. The emphasis is shifting from competition between them on the basis of price to the management of destinations in order to present a consistent range of services intended to satisfy particular types of tourist. This is reinforced by a continual (or iterative) negotiation process in which the interactions between tourists and destination managers modifies the existing tourism product. The process is similar to what occurs in other markets in which consumers' wishes as expressed by their buying behaviour (particularly their choices between alternatives), are considered by commercial organisations and by planning authorities during the development of new or improved destination services.

Patterns of tourists' destination use

The concept of core and peripheral areas introduced earlier is also useful in analysing the dispersal of visitors within the boundaries of a particular locality, whether the scale is that of a small historic city such as Canterbury or a country such as Spain. Tourists tend to cluster in core tourism areas, around Canterbury Cathedral and along its High Street, or on the Spanish coasts, while in both destinations extensive areas are much less frequented by tourists, and it is now policy to encourage use of the 'tourist-peripheral' areas. Three objectives can be identified:

1 To reduce pressure on the core area where key attractions are located by enticing visitors elsewhere.
2 Tourists represent spending power, and if they can be drawn to new zones, their presence will provide new opportunities for entrepreneurs and create additional employment. Thus, encouraging tourists to venture into the peripheries of a destination can stimulate the economy in those areas.

3 Tourist dispersal policy can also be understood as presenting 'new' features of the destination to its visitors, thus providing a platform for revised marketing programmes. In the early 1990s, Spain's tourism promotions began to emphasise its tradition, historic cities and superb landscapes of its interior. It was hoped both to attract additional visitors to Spain, and to encourage those already familiar with its bars and beaches to experience different aspects of the country.

Any effective tourist dispersal policy depends on understanding visitors' motivations, reviewing the way in which different groups of people use the area's spaces, and developing or promoting a range of attractions which will draw different types of tourists away from the existing tourist centres, but encourage them into those areas it has been decided to promote. A destination's spaces are used for different purposes by various groups of people. While a city's main shopping street and the transport termini are used by almost everyone, it is mainly residents who frequent the suburbs, and the office, administrative and manufacturing districts are used by workers and by business visitors. Tourists are found in areas which offer amusements, shopping, or cultural and historical attractions. Although these areas may overlap, the consequence is that each zone tends to have amenities catering to the needs of a specific group of users, so in order to attract tourists into a 'business' area, new elements would have to be introduced to appeal to them. For example, restaurants catering to visitors with smaller budgets and less formal requirements than business clients will be needed. In addition, it will be necessary to provide specific attractions to entice tourists into areas they have not previously frequented.

If it is not carefully planned, a dispersal policy can result in congestion and conflict because of the different usage and behavioural patterns of established and new users of spaces. For example, the open-top buses which broadcast commentaries for their tourist passengers have been a cause of complaint from Oxford's colleges. In cities such as Bath where attempts have been made to encourage visitors into attractive residential areas, resentment by its tax payers and voters has resulted. Case study B discusses how Canterbury has responded to pressures on its spaces, by improving the quality of visitors' and residents' experiences.

Case study B

Managing Canterbury's tourist spaces

Canterbury City Council, and its predecessors, have been actively involved in tourism since pilgrims were attracted in large numbers immediately after the murder of St Thomas à Becket on 29 December 1170. By 1380, when Chaucer's *Canterbury Tales* were published, there were many hostels of different grades in the city, and often the number of visitors exceeded the number of residents. The historic heritage is one of the chief reasons for foreigners to visit Britain, but its ancient buildings and streets are irreplaceable and fragile.

Canterbury is one of the most important historic cities in the country. Within the town centre there are more than 1500 listed buildings. The importance to the nation of conserving Canterbury was recognised in 1968 when the entire walled city together with the medieval suburbs was designated as a Conservation Area. More recently, the Cathedral, St Augustine's Abbey and St Martin's Church have been designated as World Heritage Sites by ICOMS, the International Committee on Monuments or Sites. Within the city there are 24 Ancient Monuments ranging from underground remains to medieval buildings. Canterbury . . . is also one of five towns in the country which have been designated as Areas of Archaeological Importance.

During the last 25 years, Canterbury has become one of the leading cities regarding conservation techniques and expertise. From 1975 to 92, nearly £5m has been spent on the repair and refurbishment of buildings in the city by the private sector aided by jointly funded grants from the city council and English Heritage under the Canterbury Town Scheme. But again, it is not always easy to achieve this sensitively. The commercial alteration of historic buildings and the 1950s and 60s development of bomb damaged sites has spoiled parts of the city centre and internal alterations (to increase floor space) can also damage the historic fabric which attracts people to the city.

(Canterbury City Centre Initiative, draft report, 1993)

Case study B *(continued)*

The District Council is responsible for an area of East Kent which includes Whitstable and Herne Bay, with a total population of 123,947 (1991 census). The historic city centre within the walls is only half a mile across, but Canterbury's shopping facilities extend to 1.9 million square feet (gross) and attract about ten million shopping visits per year from a catchment area population of 500,000, generating £115 million turnover annually. The City attracts two main classes of visitor, shoppers and heritage tourists. Although St Thomas à Becket's shrine was destroyed by Henry VIII in 1538, the Cathedral and Canterbury's historic heritage still attracts 2.25 million tourists per year. A growing number of visitors combine shopping with sightseeing, spending £51 on average. However, there is little repeat tourism business, although Canterbury is a regular tour destination for day coach excursions from London, Northern France and Belgium, benefiting from its proximity to the ferry port of Dover and its location on the A2/M2 transit corridor (Figure 1.5).

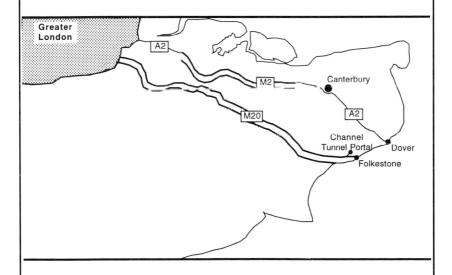

Figure 1.5 Road access to Canterbury

Case study B *(continued)*

The current concern is with the potential reduction of regional shoppers and tourist visitors (both British and European):

- Canterbury faces increased competition from improvements in other Kentish towns made more accessible by the gradual improvement in the county's roads, and the development of out-of-town shopping centres.
- The new transport infrastructure resulting from the development of the Channel Tunnel and the integrated European Community will shift the Kent transit axis to the west, and motorists will probably prefer to stay on the M20 motorway between London and Dover, rather than use the less modern A2 dual carriageway which serves as the link between Canterbury and Dover.

The Council regards it as important to provide a good experience for all visitors in the expectation that they will encourage friends and relatives to come. Their approaches include promotional activities, visitor surveys, and the development and implementation of programmes for visitor management and visitor amenity improvements. The City Local Plan (1981) recognised the pressure which large numbers of tourists placed on the attributes of the city which attracted them in the first place, and the concern is echoed in the 1994 Canterbury District Deposit Draft Local Plan. These documents form the statutory basis for the city's visitor strategy, but its implementation requires the co-ordination of many local council functions especially planning, conservation, highways and environmental health, with those undertaken by Kent County Council as strategic highway authority.

The key problem in Canterbury is the physical constraints imposed by its narrow medieval street patterns, and its buildings. The first difficulty which visitors experience is in parking, or in reaching the historic city from outlying coach and car parks, followed by the problem of locating the points of interest in the city. The city's PARC (Park and Ride in Canterbury) plan, being undertaken by the city and county councils jointly sets out the strategy for parking for cars and coaches, and pedestrian flows in

Case study B *(continued)*

the city. The aim is to keep long-term business parking out of the city centre by promoting a park and ride scheme. Central off-street parking space is earmarked for shoppers and tourists, but priced to discourage long stays, complemented by a voucher scheme and on-street parking bays to provide for residents' needs.

A quarter of Canterbury's visitors arrive by coach, although the present parking area has insufficient space for all coaches, and provides only basic catering, toilet and information facilities. Furthermore, its location is inconvenient in terms of both road and pedestrian access. Visitors arriving by coach have to walk through narrow residential streets, and they must cross a busy dual carriageway to gain access to the historic centre of Canterbury. The mid-road refuge at the pedestrian crossing cannot accommodate a complete coach party, resulting in delays, frustration and confrontation between pedestrians and motorists, and several accidents. The ultimate solution is clear, and has been accepted as a strategic goal by the council, the coach park should be relocated. However, as an interim measure until suitable land is made available, the road crossing and signage is being improved by Kent County Council. Other initiatives to improve access include a series of riverside walks linking the city centre to several new car parks, benefiting residents, those who work in the City, and its tourists and shoppers.

Tourists are unfamiliar with the city, and they tend to congregate in specific areas, particularly the Cathedral precincts and the main shopping street. After the main A2 from London to Dover was improved in the 1960s, when a bypass was constructed, the High Street was pedestrianised. This has encouraged tourists to spread further afield within the city, rather than limit their visit to the area around the Cathedral, but more pedestrianisation and additional initiatives are planned to encourage tourists to experience different areas of the City. (Figure 1.6 shows the distribution of the four main groups of city space users). In many towns, local traders have objected to the exclusion of vehicles from shopping streets during the day. Canterbury City Council

Case study B *(continued)*

justified pedestrianisation in the following way, 'The Council has (also) been implementing a policy of pedestrianisation and general street refurbishment This is not a luxury item. It makes sound economic sense to keep the town centre in good order as this is what attracts shoppers to Canterbury'.

The main attraction in Canterbury is the Cathedral, and this too experiences severe pressures from visitors, and has developed visitor management policies appropriate to a Church. The first recorded visitor-management task was to ensure that the medieval

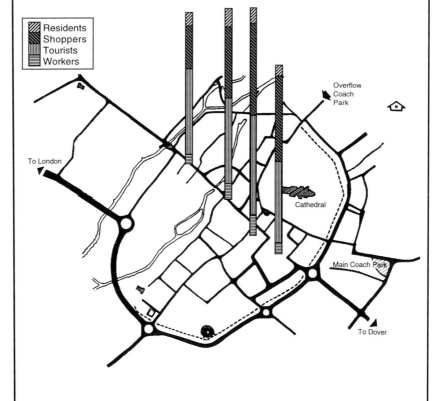

Residents
Shoppers
Tourists
Workers

Overflow
Coach
Park

To London

Cathedral

Main Coach Park

To Dover

Figure 1.6 Distribution of tourists and others around Canterbury

Case study B *(continued)*

pilgrims approached St Thomas à Becket's tomb on their knees! The modern concern is to ease the flow of visitors around the main points of interest in the Cathedral. The religious and architectural importance of the Cathedral attracts many school parties, both from Britain and abroad, and these groups were identified as a major cause of complaint by others who used the Cathedral. A scheme, 'Operation Shepherd' was developed with a number of tactics to control the entrance of groups. In the first year 1992, only 13 per cent of school groups booked their visit to the Cathedral but in 1993, 45 per cent of such groups pre-booked.

- An area near the main entrance was set aside for groups to congregate, out of the main flow.
- Groups had to be split into ten or twenty students, each accompanied by a responsible adult who was issued with an identifying badge.
- The leader was provided with a four-page A4 leaflet which explained in simple terms the main points to be seen as the group progressed in a predetermined route around the Cathedral. This includes the Nave, the site of the Martyrdom, the Crypt, the Pulpitum Steps where the advise is 'Look up and all around, noting the fan vaulting. The stone screen separated the Nave, the people's church, from the Quire, where the monks worshipped.' The visit continues through the Quire, the North Aisle and Trinity Chapel, and the South East and South West Transepts.
- The leaflet concludes the structured tour of the Cathedral at the Bookstall, and asks the leader to exit by the adjacent door. The final page of the leader's leaflet explains how future visits can be made more beneficial to students, notably by booking in advance, as immediate entry will no longer be guaranteed to un-booked groups, how to book Cathedral Guides, audio-visual facilities, and information about hiring a room where groups can eat their packed lunches.

To increase the range of attractions in Canterbury, the City Council has encouraged private projects such as Canterbury Tales,

Case study B *(continued)*

which is housed in a renovated church, and portrays the experi-ence of Chaucer's pilgrims on their journey to Canterbury. The Council has also invested in a museum explaining Canterbury's heritage more formally, and it operates a visitors' bureau in partnership with the Chamber of Trade. The tourist information centre is housed (rent-free) in a restored historic building, it serves 300,000 visitors a year, providing information leaflets about the City and the surrounding area, and it subcontracts book and souvenir sales, and a currency exchange. The council also follows a positive conservation policy, backed by grant aid to ensure the maintenance of the architectural heritage which attracts visitors.

In order to further develop Canterbury's tourism, the City Coun-cil has set up a partnership with the commercial sector, amenity groups, the Cathedral, the County Council and Christ Church College. The Canterbury City Centre Initiative aims to develop a sustainable management strategy for tourists and shoppers which complements the qualities of life of Canterbury's residents. The elements of the Canterbury City Centre Initiative are:

- The promotion of coach travel together with improved recep-tion facilities for tourists arriving by coach as an environmen-tally preferable means of visiting Canterbury than by private car.
- Pre-booked city visits for groups (particularly groups of school children), ensuring a quality service throughout the visit, an interpretation pack and a 'Shepherd' to guide groups to cultural sites.
- Improve access for mobility-impaired visitors, through park and ride and other forms of public transport.
- Communicate the economic importance of tourism to the local community.
- Co-ordinate funding of conservation, environmental improve-ments and pedestrian and traffic improvement measures.

The Canterbury City Centre Initiative includes the appointment of a Visitor Manager, and a researcher based in the College,

Case study B *(continued)*

whose role is to conduct a base study to establish the nature and extent of tourism in Canterbury, and to monitor the evolution of the City Centre Initiative.

Sources: based on interviews with Canterbury's tourism managers, and documents from the Dean and Chapter, Canterbury City Council and the Canterbury City Centre Initiative.

Suggested exercise

Conduct a pilot survey of visitor distribution in a destination accessible to you. Account for any clustering you observe, and identify under used zones. Suggest how tourists' use of the destination could be managed more effectively.

Destination systems

The discussion of destination improvements in Majorca and Canterbury indicates that an analytical framework is needed within which the many aspects of managing tourist destinations can be investigated. The interdependency of the elements which together make up tourist destinations, and the balance of effects of tourism (good or harmful) on various interest groups can best be understood from the perspective of a soft, open, systems model, (Mill and Morrison, 1985; Leiper, 1990; Checkland and Scholes, 1990). The 'soft' feature of the model is concerned with the interactions of tourists, staff and residents in tourist destination areas. The model is 'open' because it recognises the legislative, cultural and technological contexts for tourism processes. A further aspect highlighted by this analytical framework is the consequences of tourism for the area's environment and ecology. 'The relationships (between ecological and other effects and the phenomenon of mass tourism) cannot be identified if they are viewed from a narrow multidisciplinary angle.' (Krippendorf, 1987.) The 'systems' aspect of this type of model has the advantages of focusing attention on all the major inputs needed to provide tourism services, and on the outcomes of tourism processes for all groups interested in the destination. On a theoretical

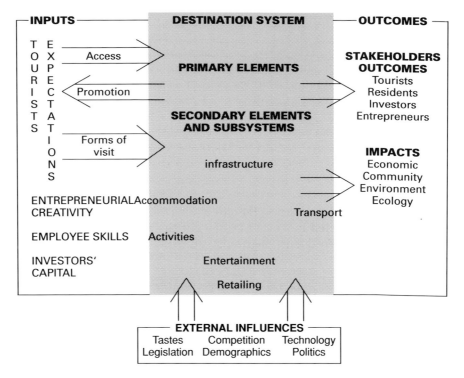

Figure 1.7 The general tourist destination systems model

level, systems theory provides a way of focusing the insights from many social sciences on destination processes and their consequences.

Figure 1.7 illustrates the components of the general tourist destination system model. All tourist destination systems consist of elements in the form of natural or primary attractions such as climate, supported by secondary features such as hotels. Destination *inputs* include managerial and technical skills, and investors' resources, and the expectations of its tourists. The general destination system is concerned with the *processes* whereby the many elements or *sub-systems* such as accommodation, entertainment and transport transforms the inputs into outputs. The quality of the tourism system's operations can also be assessed by examining the *outcomes* for each *stakeholder group*, that is the satisfaction experienced by tourists, the remuneration, work satisfaction and career development of staff, the growth of the destination can be regarded as proprietors or societal outcomes, while the benefits or problems which the tourism system creates locally are the outcomes for residents (Laws, 1991). However, the destination elements and processes are subject to *external influences* such as legislation, changes to technology, and changing demand conditions which together shape the destination's future development.

Every destination has a unique mix of characteristics which are determined by its geographical location, culture and history. These, together with the area's degree of dependency on tourism, and the industry's seasonal and structural characteristics, influence the experiences of both visitors and residents. The development of a specific systems model for each destination can clarify the relative importance of each element in a particular locality.

Systems theory argues that the efficiency of the destination's operations will be affected by changes to any of the elements of which it is composed. For effective management, three aspects need to be clearly understood:

1 The effects on outputs of any change to its inputs.
2 The ways in which its internal subsystems and processes are linked.
3 How the subsystems and processes are controlled.

Control over the quality and consistency of a system's outputs depends on an effective feedback channel between the monitoring and decision-making subsystems of the destination. These functions are based on market research to understand the expectations of visitors, and techniques to assess the impacts of tourism on the quartet of destination concerns, its society, economy, environment and ecology.

The wide range of tourists' needs during their stay is met by a variety of organisations, many are private sector, profit-oriented companies, but this diversity leads to the need for co-ordinated destination management. Typically, this role is undertaken by various governmental bodies, at national, regional and local levels. An experienced tourism administrator has pointed out that: 'Social and economic policy makers in general have not regarded tourism as important, and so state bodies responsible for tourism activity are often ill equipped to deal with its development' (Likorish, 1991a). He criticises the poor co-ordination between government departments and between the major trading sectors, arguing that tourism is usually accorded relatively low priority, and limited resources, resulting in poor co-ordination and piecemeal programmes.

This point can be taken as a criticism arising out of the systems analysis of tourist destinations, as it shows that at present few are 'systemic' in the sense of being fully integrated at a functional or managerial level. The main exceptions are theme parks. Three Disney parks in Florida, Disney World, Epcott and Disney MGM Studios, together received 30 million visitors in 1993, far exceeding the number of tourists arriving in most countries. Theme park managers enjoy several advantages over their colleagues who are responsible for other forms of tourist destination. They use one or more themes throughout the visitor experience, beginning with the name, marketing, images, and style of the destination. This high degree of control continues throughout the visitors' experience, including the design and layout of the park, its staffing and the accommodation, food service and retailing available to its clients (Grover, 1991). Theme parks represents a 'closed systems approach' to destination management where the maximum control possible is exercised over the inputs and subsystems, while the functioning and co-ordination of its elements are focused primarily on visitor satisfaction to the benefit of one stakeholder, the theme park's proprietor.

Although the experience is carefully controlled, and its elements are highly integrated, the general theme park concept has been criticised on the grounds of unsympathetic landscaping, misinformation presented on historical or cultural aspects of the theme, and because individual reaction to the destination's stimuli are replaced by programmed responses. Robinson (cited in Bramwell, 1991) argued that theme parks present an overall shallow experience which may have the additional effect of reducing visitor attendance and revenues at authentic destinations.

The various elements and subsystems of any destination are interdependent, and it is useful to think of them as set within physical and administrative boundaries. However, other organisations which are not contained within the destination's boundaries have significant roles in the area's success. The most influential of these are the tour operators and transport companies which carry out marketing, distribution and sales functions. They are usually based in the tourists' areas of origin, and their functions are considered further in Chapter 4 (and in another book in this series, Laws, forthcoming).

Conclusion

This chapter has introduced a discussion of the issues confronting destination managers and it has considered some of the approaches available to researchers interested in tourist destinations. It has examined how two major but differing destinations, Majorca and Canterbury, have recognised and responded to the particular difficulties and opportunities facing them.

Tourists themselves are a fundamental factor in the success of destinations, and Chapter 2 will provide an introductory analysis of tourists' destination choices, and the factors which influence their satisfaction during a holiday. Subsequent chapters will examine in more detail the effects of tourism and the policies destinations can implement to gain the most benefit and to minimise the harmful consequences which result from tourist activity.

Further reading

Cooper, C., Fletcher, J., Gilbert, D. and Wanhill, S. (1993) *Tourism, Principles and Practice*, London: Pitman..

Holloway, C. (1994) *The Business of Tourism*, 4th edn, London: Pitman.

Krippendorf, J. *The Holiday Makers*, Heinemann, London, 1987.

Lea, J. (1988) *Tourism and Development in the Third World*, London: Routledge.

Ryan, C. (1991) *Recreational Tourism, A Social Science Perspective*, London: Routledge.

Smith, S. L. J. (1983) *Recreation Geography*, Harlow: Longman.

West, G. (1994) *Jogging Around Majorca*, Alston Rivers, 1929, republished by Black Swan.

Suggested exercises

Examine Figure 1.8. The photographs illustrate beaches on a variety of Pacific islands at varying stages of tourism development. Consider the following questions individually, before discussing your views with your colleagues.

1 Which of these locations would you prefer to visit? What features appeal to you?
2 What would be required to develop the beaches shown in 1a and 1b to the level of tourism sophistication evident in 1c and 1d?
3 Using the systems method described in this chapter, analyse the effects on an island of carrying out the development processes you identified in answering question 2.
4 Contrast the effects of tourism on the island with those resulting from any alternative forms of economic activity.
5 Outline and justify a policy for future tourism development in your local area.

a) Western Samoa

b) Local use of a beach in Fiji

Figure 1.8 Pacific islands at varying stages of development

c) View of the beach from a hotel lanai in Waikiki

d) View from a hotel lanai in Waikiki

Figure 1.8 *(continued)*

2
Tourists' destination choices and experiences

Introduction

The decision to visit a particular destination can be seen as the individual's solution to the problem, 'Where shall I go for my holiday?' For the tourist, the decision entails a series of choices, including the budget for holidays, the time available, who to travel with, and forecasts of the satisfaction they are likely to experience at each possible destination.

Understanding the factors which underlie destination choices and the way destinations are experienced is important to managers in developing effective promotional campaigns and, since the choice of place to visit is inextricably linked to what it provides, this is also critical in determining how best to manage and develop its facilities. This chapter investigates three key issues for destination managers:

1 How tourists select a destination.
2 The factors influencing tourists' satisfaction with destination services.
3 The roles of tourism agencies in influencing their destination experiences.

Tourists' destination choices

The extensive literature analysing consumers' decision processes suggests that tourism can be distinguished from other purchases on a number of theoretical criteria:

- The interval of time which elapses between purchase and the 'consumption' of a holiday; in Britain the peak season for taking holidays is the school summer holiday months, but the highest proportion of summer package tour sales occur soon after the Christmas break.
- The high cost of holidays compared with most other purchases, for a typical family the total cost of their holiday often exceeds £1,000, representing a high proportion of their annual discretionary spending power.
- The difficulty of knowing quite what to expect in a distant, unfamiliar place.

Although the primary concern of a destination's manager is the total level of demand for holidays there, the flow of tourist arrivals represents the sum of many individuals' decisions. Their marketing efforts can stimulate increased awareness and a keener desire to visit it, but individuals' travel decisions are taken in the context of factors such as their health, the personal significance to them of holidays, and family commitments, any of which may restrict the ability of tourists to visit even those destinations which appeal strongly to them.

Health factors affecting destination choice

Individuals in Western society enjoy freedom of choice amongst the entire range of products and services affordable to them, but economists note that the decision to spend money on a specific product reduces one's ability to buy other goods and services. Holidays have now become a regular feature of many people's lifestyle. 'It is a crucial element of modern life to feel that travel and holidays are necessary. "I need a holiday" is the surest reflection of a modern discourse based on the idea that people's physical and mental health will be restored if only they can "get away" from time to time' Urry, 1990).

Good health is an important form of personal capital (Heggenhougen, 1987), thus decisions which may affect one's health have the significance of an investment in one's well-being. However, views of what is good for one's health are influenced by contemporary fashion and current scientific understanding. It has been suggested that Douglas Fairbanks and Hollywood helped to popularise the suntan, which had been regarded mainly as a form of treatment for tuberculosis. 'Going against the established wisdom which held that the fashionable body must avoid the effects of the sun, lest it be associated with the tanned labouring body, he allowed his darkened face to appear in films and the popular press'. The result was that beaches became transformed 'into a place where one gained a suntan – the hallmark of a successful holiday. For the first time sunbathing on the beach brought together large numbers of people in varying degrees of undress, legitimating the public display of the body.' (Featherstone, 1982). During the 1980s concern with the carcinogenic effects of exposure to strong sunlight became widespread, and people going on holiday to destinations where the sun was more intense were advised by tour operators, travel journalists and in destination welcome packs to minimise exposure by using strong blocker-creams, and to avoid the midday sun.

Table 2.1 Reasons for not taking a holiday

%	Reason
48	Cost
11	Time
14	Personal disability
10	Illness
5	Infirm/elderly

Source: ETB, 1985.

In contrast to the foregoing discussion, holiday taking is difficult or impossible for large numbers of people. Table 2.1 shows that although cost is the major factor inhibiting the general population from taking a vacation, some 29 per cent of the respondents to a survey enquiring why a holiday had not been taken in the previous year gave disability, age-infirmity or illness as the reason, and case study C discusses some approaches in Britain to counter difficulties in taking a holiday faced by people with special needs.

Case study C

Improving holiday access in Britain for people with special needs

Many of the problems encountered by disabled people (and those who accompany them on holiday) stem from the insensitive design of tourists spaces. Stairs, narrow doors, and bathrooms equipped only for fit people all present real barriers to wheelchair users or the elderly. Although it is very difficult to adapt the medieval buildings which are a major part of Britain's heritage attractions (Westwood, 1989), the modern hotels, restaurants and transport termini which are being added to the tourist infrastructure should be designed and equipped for easy use by disabled visitors. A study of disabled access in Britain notes a gradual improvement since 1970, but argues for further attention. '15 years ago rooms with en suite facilities or the provision of vegetarian meals might well have been thought of as special; nowadays, both are generally available . . . "special needs" are only "special" if the environment makes them so' (Baker, 1989).

Inability to participate in holidays is a serious matter, for the disadvantaged individual, those who care for him or her, and for society generally. Being unable to travel or to stay temporarily away from one's routine surroundings:

Is an isolating factor, which can also undermine health. . . . Holidays, far from being a frivolous activity, are part of living the fullest life possible . . . they can give the carer the strength to carry on or the opportunity to meet new friends. They can give the frail and elderly or those with mobility problems a welcome change from a perhaps restrictive or isolated routine.

(Baker, 1989)

The positive benefit gained from holiday-taking extends beyond the time spent away from home. The involvement and enjoyment starts with planning and anticipating the break, continues with the enjoyment of holidays, and persists after returning home.

Planning and arranging holidays for disabled people requires

Case study C *(continued)*

reliable, detailed information, and ease in making the arrangements. Selling one disabled person a holiday typically produces several clients, and consequently the English Tourist Board (ETB) recommends that access information should be included in hotel brochures and attraction leaflets, and that group organisers should be encouraged to contact a venue to specify the requirements of disabled clients prior to the visit.

The potential British market of additional holiday-takers for whom access is difficult includes 10.3 million pensioners. Retired people are more likely than the general population to take two or more holidays. They are less likely to go abroad, and more likely to take off-peak breaks. Their average stay is six nights, one longer than average, and they tend to use the more profitable serviced accommodation in preference to self-catering arrangements, and the over-75 age group is forecast to increase by 70 per cent in the early years of next century.

The argument is twofold: people should be free to take whatever holiday they like, but any problem encountered by those with disabilities is likely to reduce their propensity for future leisure participation, with detrimental effects on their quality of life. However, the elimination of discriminatory provision, policies and attitudes depends on better understanding. The author of the ETB report discussed above has advocated an objective assessment of accessibility and the development of marketing standards for disabled people. 'Drawing up international minimum standards is one solution, but design solutions to improve access to buildings and leisure or sporting amenities is a better way forward than legislating for ramp access' (Baker, 1989). Table 2.2 summarises the key recommendations to improve access to destinations for disabled visitors.

Sources: based on articles cited.

Case study C *(continued)*

Table 2.2 Key factors in improving destinations for disabled visitors' access

---

* Improvements in transport
* Integrating special facilities such as ramps into the design
* Objective assessments of accessibility
* Consultation with organisations representing disabled people when planning
* Training for architects to cater for the 'wider average'
* Increased information about access in promotional literature
* The development of internationally agreed standards

Based on: Baker, 1989 and Brown, 1991.

Suggested exercise

Consider the problems which one or more of the following tourists are likely to encounter when visiting a destination familiar to you, and suggest relevant improvements:

* a frail, elderly couple
* a wheelchair user
* a blind person travelling alone.

Involvement and freedom in destination choice

Holidays represent a period of time when the individual is relatively free from everyday constraints, and is able to indulge his or her wishes. They also represent a deliberate purchase, in which one's limited financial resources are invested in buying time in a specific destination, implying both that the tourist cannot visit alternative destinations during that holiday, and that he or she has chosen not to spend money and time on alternative products. Consumers' degrees of interest and 'involvement' in purchasing particular products or services range from *low* to *high*, and Cohen (1968) defined involvement as 'a state of arousal that a person experiences in regard to consumption related activity.' Involvement is likely to be high when the purchase has functional and symbolic significance, and entails some financial risk (Asseal, 1987). Four aspects of holidays indicate that many tourists experience a high degree of involvement in choosing their destination.

1 Holidays are expensive.
2 They are complex both to purchase and experience.
3 There is a risk that the destination will not prove satisfying.
4 The destination reflects the holidaymaker's personality.

The significance of regarding holidays as a high involvement purchase is that considerable care will be invested in the choice of destination, with potential tourists undertaking detailed and extended study of brochures, reading and watching holiday advertising, and visiting travel agencies for advice to identify suitable places to visit.

For some people however, the decision about which destination to visit is so circumscribed by the purpose for which travel is undertaken that it scarcely qualifies as a choice, examples include travel for family reasons, or to attend business meetings. At the other extreme, the decision to go on holiday opens up a choice from the entire spectrum of vacation resorts. At an intermediate level, a requirement for specific destination attributes limits the choice, for example the holiday-maker who wishes to go powder skiing is restricted to a limited range of mountain resorts. Table 2.3 illustrates the hierarchy of destination choice freedoms.

Table 2.3 Degrees of freedom in holiday destination choices

Circumscribed destination
    Visit to family
    Business travel

Specific requirements
    Preferred activities
    Preferred climate

General restrictions
    Budget available
    Time available

Tourists faced with relative freedom in their choice of destination have a variety of factors to consider. Figure 2.1 adapts the decision tree method to investigate how a specific destination is chosen. The first decision to be made is whether to take a holiday at all. Spending on holidays is discretionary, and as Martin and Mason (1993) have pointed

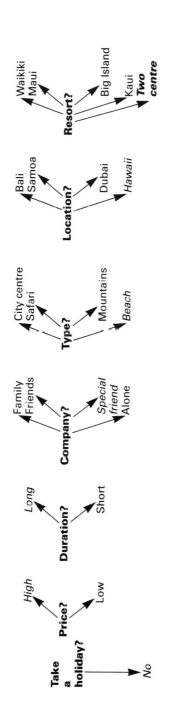

Figure 2.1 Destination selection tree

Note: Italics trace the elements of the final destination selection decisions discussed in the text.

out, activities are cut at different rates when finance is tight, for example during a recession, or when a family has young children. Another factor in deciding whether to take a holiday is one's physical state of health, or that of family members, while the pressure of other activities such as work or study may limit the time available.

Once the decision has been made to take a holiday, other general decisions remain, including the holiday budget, the duration of the holiday and the question of with whom to go. These choices represent progressive 'branches' of the decision tree, and once taken, each of these decisions narrows the range of destinations remaining under consideration. Some may be eliminated because they are too expensive, or too remote for the length of time available. Others may be unsuitable for mobility-impaired holiday companions. The next level of the decision tree offers a choice spectrum embracing city breaks, mountains or a beach holiday.

The beach holiday branch itself presents the potential holidaymaker with a choice between many specific destinations. However, if the tourist wishes to visit an exotic long-haul destination, the choice, although still wide becomes more specific. Destinations such as Bali, Dubai and Hawaii are substitutes for each other in that they offer the holidaymaker similar core benefits, being exotic destinations with generally excellent climates, beaches and hotels, and interesting scenery and cultures, located in (or near) the tropics. The choice between them is determined by what the tourist knows of their secondary features such as accommodation, attractions and accessibility. If the holidaymaker chooses Hawaii, he or she still has to select one of the five main islands, or a combination of them, although most first-time visitors stay in Waikiki. An alternative method of understanding how people select their holiday destination is to analyse the opportunity set from which they can make their choice. Stabler (1990) has defined the concept as those holiday opportunities which are available to a customer at any point in time.

Joint holiday decisions

Many people take their vacations in the company of friends, or with their family. Hunt (1978), discussed a study by Bonfield which investigated the differing responsibilities of spouses in four types of family purchasing decisions. The wife's influence was strongest when choosing household and children's consumption items, while the husband selected garden or motoring items. The choice of gifts was an intermediate case, either partner taking the lead depending on the situation, while the family holiday was largely a matter for joint decisions.

Davis (1976) has shown that families reach a joint decision about important choices by one of two major processes. Consensus happens when the family members agree about their goals (for example, needing relaxation after a stressful year, or a shared desire to enjoy a change of climate and scenery). However, when family members have differing goals, some wanting to holiday in a centre offering varied night life, others preferring to stay with relatives in a quiet rural setting, the strength of the family unit leads to a compromise, or accommodation. Each family member plays a role in the negotiation, based variously on their expertise, experience or their negotiating skills and status in the group. *Consensual decisions* are reached through problem solving strategies, while *accommodation* results either from persuasion, or by bargaining various benefits.

The balance of decision roles between man and wife varies at different life-cycle stages. In a survey of 9,000 visitors leaving Florida, Fodness (1992) found that young couples shared equally in gathering brochures, but when they became parents the woman was most likely to perform this task, which senior couples again shared equally. The actual choice of destination was a joint activity for 93 per cent of senior couples, and 88 per cent of young couples.

Studies such as these have implications for the way in which destination literature is distributed, as well as for the images and texts it contains. Since women with children are the most likely ones to collect information, effective distribution entails placing brochures in outlets which are easily accessible to them, and advertising on the media which they are most likely to read or notice.

The social context of holiday-taking is also a factor in behaviour at the destination.

> The behavior of visitors at interpretation centers, for example, does not arise in isolation but is guided by the culture, community and age group of which each individual is a member. A 15 year old male may behave differently at a local historic site depending on whether he arrives with parents, church group, street group or girl friend.
>
> (Machlis and Field, 1992)

This is significant for the 'atmosphere' in a destination, because many tour operators' segmentation strategy is based on their clients' age, special holiday packages being developed and promoted for young people or the elderly. As a consequence, in many countries including Britain, Spain and Florida, certain resorts have a perceived image as being for 'the elderly', while others are regarded as a good setting for lager and riots.

Tourists' satisfaction with destination services

The general tourist destination systems model discussed in Chapter 1 (Figure 1.7) indicated that tourists should be regarded as inputs into the system, and that their experiences there form the basis of their satisfaction outcomes. Tourism can be characterised as a specialised consumption activity, unique in that people displace themselves from familiar environments and voluntarily invest their time and money in making a journey to somewhere less familiar, where they undertake a range of activities before returning home.

Another characteristic of holidays is that services rather than goods are purchased. Kotler (1982) has defined services as: 'an activity that one party can offer to another that is essentially intangible and does not result in the ownership of anything'. In other words, the people who work to create and deliver touristic experiences have extensive contact with their clients. Anecdotal evidence supports this view, people often discuss the rapport (or otherwise) which they struck up with the waiter, barman, or courier during a holiday. The quality of these relationships, and the style of service delivery are just as significant in tourists' satisfaction and enjoyment as the efficiency with which the services are performed. Table 2.4 summarises the main characteristics of tourist destination services.

The way in which tourists experience a destination can be understood as a set of phases beginning with the development of an intention to

Table 2.4 Service characteristics of tourist destinations

---
* Production and enjoyment of services coincide in time and location
* Tourists participate in the creation of the services they purchase
* There is a high degree of interaction between tourists and destination staff
* Staff from many organisations contribute to each visitor's destination experiences
* Destination experiences are unique to each visitor
* Tourists cannot 'sample' the destination before arriving for their holiday
* Services such as bed nights and meals cannot be stored for sale at a later date

---

Based on: Cowell, 1986; Gummesson, 1988; Laws, 1992; and Parasuraman *et al.*, 1988.

Table 2.5 Influences on tourists' destination satisfaction

Phase of holiday	Activity	Influencers	Destination or tour operator controlled?
Pre-travel	1 Purchase decisions	Advertising Brochures NTO information	D, T T D

	2 Planning	Opinions of:
		  travel agent
		  travel writers
			?
			n

	3 Anticipation	friends	n
Journey and arrival	4 Travel	Airline staff Airport staff	n ?
	5 Transfer to hotel	Immigration/customs Baggage handlers Courier	D D T
Destination stay	6 Accommodation	Hotel staff Restaurant staff	? ?
	7 Catering	Courier Coach driver	T ?
	8 Entertainment	TIC Guide books	D n

	9 Excursions	Casual contacts with:
		  residents
		  other visitors
			n
			n

After return home	10 Recollection	Photographs video souvenirs discussion with friends travel writing advertising brochures	n ? n n ? D, T T

Note: D = Destination; T = Tour operator; ? = Either; n = No control by either destination or tour operator.

visit it, continuing with the experiences of a variety of services during their stay at the destination, and culminating in their memories of the destination after returning home. Table 2.5 summarises these phases in the form of a flow chart, distinguishing between the ability of the destination or the tour operator to influence visitors' expectations or experiences at each stage.

Destination and tour operator managers need to know what their clients regard as the components of a satisfying tourism experience in order to provide it effectively. In a sense, tourists 'measure' the quality of services which they receive against the expectations they formed ahead of travel when they selected, purchased and then anticipated their journey (Laws, 1986). The process by which consumers understand quality is now regarded as a comparison of the service standards expected against their perceptions of what they experience. The outcome of the evaluation process may be viewed as an operational definition of service quality, implying that the critical aspects of quality are not just inherent in the properties of the service itself (Garvin, 1988). Quality is also a function of the consumer's experiences and the personal values which govern their expectations (Engel *et al.*, 1986).

A weak link in the formation of expectations is created by many tour operators and destination agencies who tend to exaggerate the uniqueness or the high quality of the services they offer, thereby increasing the likelihood of disappointment, a problem which is exacerbated by the lack of co-ordination between the many organisations providing services to tourists within a destination. Case study D examines some of the approaches to destination quality control adopted by the Wales Tourist Board.

Case study D

Tourist-customer care in Wales

As preparation for its strategy to prepare Welsh tourism for the conditions it will face in the twenty-first century, the Wales Tourist Board (WTB), commissioned a series of studies and discussion papers dealing with the major aspects of tourism in the country, which were circulated to the industry's members for comment.

In one paper, *Tourism 2,000, A Perspective for Wales*, Wanhill provided a framework, and commented that tourists have rising expectations of the facilities and service delivery systems. 'Competing on quality ... means delivering consistent good service promptly, courteously and with intelligence and enthusiasm. In many instances quality of service delivery can make up for defects in the product, to put it simply, people like to go where they feel welcome.' In Consultative Paper No. 8, Coleman (1992) discusses customer care issues in detail.

Case study D *(continued)*

Complaints to the WTB about all tourism services in the country are rare, and the rate is fairly constant, at between 500 and 600 a year. The WTB categorises them into seven types, and the proportion received in each category in 1992 is given in Table 2.6.

Table 2.6 Reasons for tourists' complaints in Wales in 1992

%	
28	Accommodation
23	Cleanliness
10	Attitudes towards tourists
7	Service
7	Food
2	Value for money
22	Miscellaneous
	(complaints about cancellation, misrepresentation, safety, noise and so on. This category had increased from 10% in 1988)

A total of less than 600 complaints may seem too few to merit attention other than a direct response to each complainant, but several studies have observed an iceberg effect linked to unsatisfactory purchases. For each dissatisfied customer who complains, many more, perhaps twenty times the number of people, do not register a formal complaint. This is significant in two ways:

1 There is no opportunity to put things right for the non-complainers.
2 Dissatisfied customers tell their friends and colleagues about their bad experience with greater frequency than satisfied customers discuss their enjoyable experiences. Therefore, there is a real impact on potential visitors who hear directly about the negative aspects of a particular holiday destination from people they know.

About a quarter of a million visitor-beds are available in Wales. The WTB was the first regional tourist authority in Britain to

Case study D *(continued)*

introduce a system of voluntary inspection for tourist accommodation. The WTB inspection scheme is voluntary because the British Government had adopted a view that it is unnecessary to provide statutory inspection and registration. At its peak, about 6,500 organisations providing tourist accommodation participated in the scheme, but the figure had fallen to 5,000 by 1992. The classifying system, crowns for hotels, and dragons for self-catering, is regarded as confusing to visitors, because the award of crowns does not equate to quality levels.

The scheme consists of physical inspection for compliance to published standards, and a code of practice which has slight variances for each sector. Inspection has been extended to include a subjective assessment of service delivery standards, with the benefit that visitors can distinguish between different accommodation businesses on the basis of the quality band to which they had been allocated as a result of the inspection process.

Less than 55 per cent of all accommodation space in Wales is managed by participants of the inspection scheme, and consequently the WTB is unable to influence the product or service standards offered by approximately half of the businesses providing accommodation to visitors to the destination. Similarly, the WTB is only able to endorse half of what is available but satisfactory standards provide the hotel, guest house or caravan park operator with access to the WTB's extensive listings.

The classification scheme was referred to the Office of Fair Trading (OFT), because hotel operators outside it were not permitted to participate in the WTB's marketing programmes, and were not listed in official tourist publications. The OFT report vindicated the scheme, although in the report, it stopped short of recognising the policy objective of consumer protection which was central to the WTB's purpose.

The final version of the Tourism 2,000 Strategy document states: 'The Board reaffirms its policy that participation in WTB accreditation schemes is a prerequisite of direct or indirect marketing support.' It also recognises the need for: 'consumer research to establish the significance of quality assurance schemes

Case study D *(continued)*

---

in the decision making process. The research will also examine the product expectations which the consumer gains from such schemes' (Wanhill, 1994).

Sources: based on Wales Tourist Board documents.

Suggested exercise

Summarise the exchange of views expressed by both parties during a discussion between a Tourist Board's representative and a hotel manager who does not wish to participate in the area's voluntary grading scheme for accommodation.

Tourists' destination recommendations

A key factor in managing tourism for quality is to understand what satisfaction clients anticipate from the purchase of a visit to destination. Consumer decision-taking represents a choice between alternative allocations of time and funds, and such choices can cause anxiety about the correctness of the decision taken. This points to a significant difference between goods and services. One of the themes explored in marketing literature is the importance of trials – a means by which the consumer gains more detailed information about an intended purchase and forms an opinion of its compatibility to his or her own needs and preferences. The subject of interest in trials is typically a low involvement, frequently-purchased FMCG (fast moving consumer goods) such as breakfast cereals, or colas where the benefits and features of competing brands are rather similar.

In the case of tourism purchases, the trial stage of decision making has received rather less attention from theorists. Destinations cannot be 'sampled' by potential visitors in the way that cereals can be tried in small quantities, or a car can be taken for a test drive. Instead, the tourist's decision to purchase a particular package holiday is based on information contained in brochures and what friends report about their experiences, and this is the basis for a contractual obligation resulting in the holiday being taken. Often, however, there is a significant time interval between booking a holiday and arrival in the destination, and during this period there is time for further reflection or reading, but without the option for the tourist to change his or her mind once the deposit has been paid to a travel agent.

Tourists themselves are a dynamic factor in a destination's development. The majority of visitors have experience of other resorts, and it is inevitable that they will make comparisons between the facilities, attractions and service standards of alternative destinations. This comparison process takes two main forms:

1 Tourists discuss their experiences with destination managers and staff, stressing features which they had found pleasing or dissatisfying. Their preferences and dislikes act as strong economic signals to entrepreneurs, and many resorts conduct formal market research to identify their actual or potential points of advantage from customers' perspectives, as a basis for decisions about further development.
2 After returning home, tourists often discuss their experiences and opinions with their friends and colleagues, thus influencing many potential holidaymakers' choice of destination.

Understanding tourists' destination activities

Tourism is defined as a temporary activity, and consequently tourists want to make the most of the time spent at their destination. Furthermore, the destination area is relatively unfamiliar to visitors, and generally they want to undertake a variety of activities during their stay. The way in which people allocate available time between alternative activities can be investigated by time budgeting techniques. Figure 2.2 shows a notional time budget for a tourist on holiday in a beach resort. It distinguishes his or her allocation of time on four different days, according to the visit phase and the state of the weather, and may be contrasted with the more structured and routine way in which residents are likely to use their time in the same area.

Tourists tend to cluster in specific zones of the destination area, and to experience only limited aspects of its culture. The consequences can be seen in the proliferation of tourist-related businesses such as shops and amusements in those areas.

In urban centres where administrative, cultural and social activities predominate, tourism is superimposed on the established patterns of

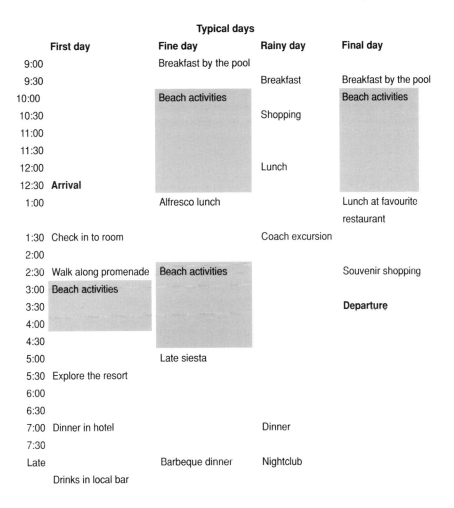

	First day	**Fine day**	**Rainy day**	**Final day**
		Typical days		
9:00		Breakfast by the pool		
9:30			Breakfast	Breakfast by the pool
10:00		Beach activities		Beach activities
10:30			Shopping	
11:00				
11:30				
12:00			Lunch	
12:30	**Arrival**			
1:00		Alfresco lunch		Lunch at favourite restaurant
1:30	Check in to room		Coach excursion	
2:00				
2:30	Walk along promenade	Beach activities		Souvenir shopping
3:00	Beach activities			
3:30				**Departure**
4:00				
4:30				
5:00		Late siesta		
5:30	Explore the resort			
6:00				
6:30				
7:00	Dinner in hotel		Dinner	
7:30				
Late		Barbeque dinner	Nightclub	
	Drinks in local bar			

Figure 2.2 Time budget for a beach holiday

human life. Similarly, those who promote a place for its touristic values may be competing with other promotional agencies disseminating different images and attempting to attract different users to the same space. For example, one place may be 'sold' as a shopping centre for the regional population, as an international tourist destination, and as a cultural centre for its inhabitants. Understanding that a destination is multi-purchased, and that its space users have only non-exclusive rights of consumption, explains the congestion often encountered in tourist centres, and the conflicting interests of differently motivated visitors and residents (Jansen-Verbeke, 1988).

Forms of tourism and tourists' destination experiences

An alternative perspective on destination choice to the rational logic of the decision tree model (Figure 2.1) focuses on the easy availability of package holidays. Travel agencies regularly display 'Late Offers' in their windows. On one day in early summer 1994, a South London agency featured a choice of fifty destinations, including the following seven-night holidays in standard tourist grade hotels departing from Gatwick during the following week:

- Lido di Jésolo   £279 per person, twin share
- Albufero   £169 per person, twin share
- San Francisco   £280 per person, twin share

From this perspective, the destination itself may become a subsidiary choice, since the tourist is effectively choosing on the basis of price from what is offered by retail agencies and tour operators. Increasingly, the range of destinations is determined by tour operators and retailers objectives of growth, cost reduction, unit profitability or increased market share, and their relative negotiating strength compared to the destination. Cohen (1972) has distinguished four forms of tourist, 'drifters', 'explorers', 'individual mass tourists' and 'organised mass tourists'. They vary in independence depending on the degree of institutionalisation of their holiday, mass tourists tending to rely most heavily on a holiday company and its staff.

Tourists arriving in packaged groups have much of their time organised by their courier. They are conducted to predetermined parts of the destination, following in the wake of many previous groups, and encountering cultural or other organisations which have developed a routine for receiving visiting groups. Other repeat visitors grow increasingly familiar with the destination and venture into less visited places. In doing so, their experience of the area changes. 'Tourists as place consumers have extremely varied patterns of holiday behaviour, intensities of use of the product, previous histories of experience with it and sets of motives for the visit' (Jansen-Verbeke, 1988).

A result of intensive tourist use of a particular zone is a 'dilution' of local culture. Reynolds (1993) has documented the westernisation of food as an aspect of tourism resulting in cultural dilution. In Bali, the average number of dishes offered in restaurants increased from 57 in 1988 to 73 in 1992. However, the proportion of Balinese dishes fell from 52 per cent to 16 per cent in the same period. Commenting on this Reynolds observed that: 'Food is often the last area of authenticity affordable by the tourist on a regular basis.' Of tourists interviewed, 58 per cent had expected a greater selection of indigenous dishes, and many reported they were bored by the repetition of Nasi Goreng and Satay. Changing menus also affect the local population, while none ate in the more expensive tourist restaurants, 64 per cent reported to Reynolds that their children had developed a preference for Western foods, especially pizzas and hamburgers.

Tourism intermediaries

The more exotic the destination, the more its visitors depend on the services of a guide. It is not only a case of language barriers, the visitor is often unaware of all there is to see, and is uncertain how to behave in social settings, or when near the local wild life. The guide's role has been the subject of critical, despairing and jocular attention by travel writers through the ages, many agree that the best guides had two essential attributes, an understanding of local customs and places, and an awareness of his or her client's interests. Traditionally, the guide was thus an agent for the client, easing, facilitating and making more satisfactory arrangements than the client could on his or her own. However, the guide's purpose was essentially mercenary, the client was charged a fee for services and many travellers' memoirs reveal suspicions that the guide was making lucrative but covert deals with local traders. Knowledge of local customs and languages was held suspect when away from the guide's immediate area, and descriptions of the resultant tensions in the relationships between guide and client provide some of the best passages in travel writing (Bell, 1907, republished in 1985).

The traditional roles of the guide remain important features of travel, but now they are undertaken by a variety of contemporary travel intermediaries. The most common modern form of guiding is a courier who has responsibility for a group of travellers during an inclusive holiday. Travellers in groups represent a source of revenue for the courier, generating commission from their purchases and activities. The courier benefits financially from keeping the group together and

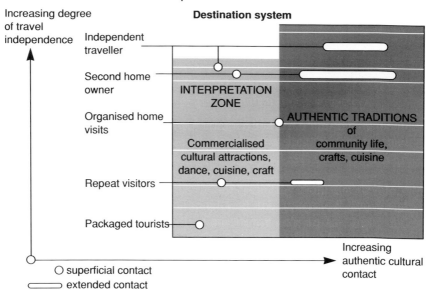

Figure 2.3 Forms of tourism and degree of cultural contact

taking them to places where a commission has been arranged, while the clients benefit from being escorted to the activities and areas which experience has shown is of interest to them.

Figure 2.3 draws together some elements discussed in this chapter, suggesting that tourists' experiences of an area's culture or its ecology are largely dependent on the form in which their visits are organised. The four forms of tourism, independent travel, repeat visits, organised tours and second-home ownership all represent valid ways of experiencing a destination. They appeal to differently motivated travellers and to those making different financial and time commitments, but they result in different outcomes for tourists and their host communities. Independent travellers, or those who own second homes are most likely to develop a deep contact with local residents while other visitors experience superficial contacts, or are exposed to staged, commercialised aspects of its features, dance, music, cuisine, crafts, and wildlife.

One manifestation is the wish of many visitors to meet locals, to sample their way of life, to observe their domestic and work practices and to participate (at least as spectators) in their ceremonials. As tourism becomes established in an area, various businesses are established providing opportunities to see local dances and traditional ways of life. These are the 'front regions' of destinations, spaces created specifically for tourists, and usually offered to them on a commercial basis (MacCannell, 1976).

> Tourists who are in search of an authentic experience ... hope to penetrate behind the front show settings into a back space where the real day to day living takes place. Tourists commonly believe they have penetrated back settings of society when they are really being shown a staged facsimile.
>
> (Goffman, 1959)

The contrast which is often drawn between travellers and tourists is relevant in understanding what outcomes are likely to result. 'The traveller was active, he went strenuously in search of people, of adventure, of experience. The tourist is passive, he expects interesting things to happen to him. He goes sight seeing' (Ritchie and Zins, 1978). Boorstin wrote of a style of sightseeing he called 'cultural mirage', and argued that whereas pilgrims are motivated to visit a place where an event of religious importance actually occurred, tourists expect experiences to be arranged for their convenience, and are often unwilling to accept uncomfortable local conditions.

> (the tourist often remains) out of contact with foreign people in the very act of sightseeing them. They keep the natives in quarantine while the tourist in air conditioned comfort views them through a picture window. They are the cultural mirages now found at tourist oases everywhere.
>
> (Boorsten, 1975)

As tourism develops, it is increasingly rare for visitors to be invited into the private and authentic social spaces that stimulate tourists consciousness. (Figure 2.4 illustrates how the Tonga Cultural Centre presents traditional crafts in a specially constructed exhibition centre where visitors can also learn about local cultural traditions, and contrasts this with a local entrepreneur's approach. Case study E discusses aspects of tourism and cultural interpretation in Tonga).

Jubenville *et al.* (1987) have discussed the methods of interpretation suitable for outdoor sites such as nature reserves. These include talks, demonstrations, and guided walks where visitors benefit from the personal services of a member of staff. However, many destination organisations employ non-local staff who have the advantage of being able to communicate with visitors, and are closer to them in cultural terms than the local residents. As an example, a ground handler in the United Arab

a) Demonstration and explanation of Tapa cloth making

b) Explanation of traditional woodcarving

Figure 2.4 Interpreting Tongan culture

c) Model boats offered for sale at a local beauty spot

d) Conclusion of visit to Tongan Cultural Centre (participating in the Khava ceremony)

Figure 2.4 *(continued)*

Emirates markets short desert excursions by four-wheel drive vehicle. The programme provides tourists with the excitement of an afternoon spent driving through dunes at high speed, and a visit to a stable of racing camels. It concludes with a barbecue under the night sky. The firm selects its guides primarily for their driving skill, and many are young Europeans. The information they can give about the desert is limited to their own knowledge and to hearsay, such as warnings not to wander off at night, and not to eat any of the plants, 'because some are dangerous'.

Another approach to destination interpretation is to provide self-guiding facilities giving independent visitors information relevant to particular sites. The problems with this solution are judging what level of detail and explanation to provide, and how to present it. Information boards are a common method of conveying information, but they may be intrusive on the landscape, or they can cause congestion as people congregate around them. Audio-tape facilities can overcome language difficulties, but these require people to progress around the area at a pre-decided rate and order. This can have the benefit of controlling visitor flows, but can lead to frustration if the pace does not suit elderly or very young visitors. An alternative method is to provide regular (or rolling) video films explaining aspects of the destination in a theatre show before people tour the facilities. Case study E, on Tonga, shows how this isolated Pacific Kingdom introduces its visitors to key aspects of its culture and traditions.

Case study E

Tourism in Tonga

Tonga is described in its promotional literature as 'a miniature kingdom in the heart of Polynesia'. It is one of the world's few remaining constitutional monarchies and the government's policy is to stimulate economic development for its 96,000 citizens while preserving ancient traditions. The economy is based on agriculture, the cottage-manufacturing of handicrafts and tourism.

Tonga offers its visitors an equable climate, verdant scenery and an attractive culture and heritage in which they feel safe. In 1991, Tonga received 22,007 international tourist arrivals. The limited

Case study E *(continued)*

Table 2.7 Origins of visitors to Tonga

Market	1990	1991	1992
New Zealand	4,840	5,566	6,661
USA	4,540	4,991	5,029
Australia	3,519	3,536	3,645
Germany	1,118	1,531	1,861
Other European	1,302	1,190	1,252
UK	755	896	612
Fiji	1,039	1,121	1,129
Other Pacific	1,024	914	866
Japan	542	741	756
Other countries	2,240	1,521	1,129
Total	20,919	22,007	22,940

Source: 1992 Tourism Council of the South Pacific survey.

international-standard accommodation reflects the small scale of its visitor industry and constrains its further development, but Tonga's geographical isolation is the critical reason for the small number of visitors. Table 2.7 shows the origins of Tonga's tourists.

In 1991 a new international air terminal was opened in Tonga, and the government launched an international airline, in the hope

Table 2.8 Air access to Tonga (Fua'amotu): May 1991

Airline	From	To	Frequency	Seats
Samoan Air	Pago Pago	Vava'u	2-weekly	20
Royal Tongan	Auckland	Fua'amotu	2 weekly	136
	Nadi	Fua'amotu	1 weekly	136
Polynesian	Apia	Sydney/Auckland	1 weekly	50
Air New Zealand	Auckland	Fua'amotu	1 weekly	106
	Auckland	USA	1 weekly	204
	Weekly seats available on Tongan flights			652

Based on: *Matangi-Tonga*, Tonga, June, 1993.

Case study E *(continued)*

of increasing the nation's share of Pacific area tourist arrivals. Fua'amotu airport is now able to take two 767s a week, and an unlimited number of 737 aircraft, but it is not able to provide for long-haul services direct to the USA, and because of the limited services its air traffic control above 10,000 feet is provided from Nadi. There are six airfields in Tonga, but none of the others are able to accept jet aircraft. In 1992, arrivals had increased to 22,940.

In early 1993 six international airlines served Tonga: Air Pacific, Air New Zealand, Polynesian, Royal Tongan, Samoa Air and Hawaiian Airlines. Due to financial problems, Hawaiian terminated its services to Tonga in March. These carriers provide only a limited number of seats for passengers embarking or disembarking in Tonga, as their main purpose is to service their own State. After Tonga launched its own scheduled airline, both Polynesian and Air Pacific reduced the frequency of their services, in part because of protectionist measures at Fua'amotu favouring Royal Tongan Airlines.

The termination of Polynesian Airlines' Friday service was particularly damaging to tourism because of the disruption it caused to a popular and widely advertised route network which had allowed tourists to island-hop around the South Pacific, and enabled tour operators to package several island groups on one itinerary. The reason was that an Air Service agreement between Tonga and New Zealand required each government to designate one airline to operate the route between Tonga and Auckland. When it was drawn up in 1980, the Tongan Government granted their rights to Polynesian Airlines as there was no expectation that Tonga would operate its own airline. After Royal Tongan started service to Auckland, the New Zealand authorities challenged Polynesian's 5th freedom rights to pick up passengers in Tonga.

The Tonga Visitors Bureau (TVB) has produced several leaflets explaining how visitors should behave in the context of Tonga's culture. The 'yacht arrival leaflet' makes specific references to Sunday, clothing and plantations.

Case study E *(continued)*

- Sunday is a day of quiet and worship. Please observe our day of worship with respect. Loud noises, boisterous parties or working (especially with power tools) are not allowed on Sundays . . .
- While European bathing attire is tolerated on some beaches, nudity (including topless lady's wear) [*sic*] is not allowed. This applies to what is worn on the deck of yachts when in public view, as well. When in town, visitors are encouraged to dress properly. Men must, by law, wear shirts in public.
- When you are wandering about on the land, please understand that all of the land belongs to someone and all of the coconut trees, fruit trees and food plants are someone's personal property. If you want some food you can buy it from the people who own the land but do not take it, not even coconuts, without asking permission first. This is important as in our culture, stealing food is a social disgrace.

Another leaflet promotes the Tonga Home Visit System, introduced to facilitate personal contact between tourists and residents. Application must be made through the TVB office, which provides detailed information on how to find the hosts' home, explaining that many Tongan houses do not have a street address. The leaflet advises visitors about what to expect when they visit their host family at home:

- You take off your shoes at the entrance before entering the house. Your host will usher you into the guest room where you may sit on the floor or chairs if available. A cup of tea or cold drinks may be served but that is not normal in Tongan custom . . .
- It should be noted that most Tongan families have constructed western style houses. . . . Instead of a Tongan style guest room a western style living room may be used for friendly conversation with the family. Traditionally, Tongan houses (*fales*) are built of coconut wood and plaited coconut leaves and are generally a breezy structure. But now almost all houses are constructed of wood and concrete

Case study E *(continued)*

western style due to their durability during cyclones and
storms.

- Do not be disappointed if you cannot find anyone in the
  Tongan family wearing their traditional costume. The
  Tongan costume is usually worn to ceremonies, church or
  special occasions. . . . Although you may find some members
  of the family wearing the *tupenu* (or the skirt-like wrap
  around) most Tongans wear western style clothing . . .

Many traditional handicrafts can be purchased in the Kingdom of
Tonga. A leaflet explains that most products are based on woven
tapa cloth made from the bark of the mulberry tree.

The sound of wooden mallets beating out lengths of tapa cloth
is one of the most familiar sounds of Tonga. From early morning until sunset throughout the Island kingdom women gather
in their homes or at the village communal tapa house to assist
each other in tapa making. . . . After further processing, traditional patterns are painted on each individual piece of cloth.
Both tapa and mats woven from pandanus leaves are customary gifts at weddings, births and funerals.

A National Cultural Centre has been established to provide
Tongans and visitors with the opportunity to learn about many
aspects of the culture, and most commercial tours around the main
island feature a visit to the Centre (Figure 2.4). It has an educational centre where Tongans are trained in traditional crafts, and
an amphitheatre for large folklore displays. A series of exhibition
halls designed to reflect the traditional architecture of the
Kingdom house Tongans displaying and explaining crafts such as
tapa making, mat weaving, canoe making, and wood carving. The
grounds of the Centre are planted with indigenous species which
also provide the raw materials for handicrafts, and are also
explained to tourists.

Visitors are greeted in an exhibition centre which presents a
history of Tonga, and are then guided through the craft halls
where they can observe the processes and discuss the work

Case study E *(continued)*

involved. Typically, a visit lasts an hour or so and concludes with an exhibition of traditional dances by a small group of Tongans, who also invite their guests to participate with them as they perform a traditional welcoming ceremony, and everyone drinks from a large kava bowl before visitors exit via a shop where books about Tonga's culture and history, as well as souvenirs made by the Centre's craftsmen, can be purchased.

Sources: based on discussions with tourism managers in Tonga, and Tongan Visitor Bureau leaflets.

Suggested exercise

Draft a leaflet for visitors from a remote traditional culture, explaining to them how to behave as tourists in your locality.

Conclusion

It has now been established that a variety of factors influence the decision to visit a particular destination. The way in which the visit is structured and organised is also a significant influence on tourists' understanding and enjoyment of the destination. The four forms of tourism discussed previously, independent travel, organised home visits, repeat visits, packaged tours and second-home ownership appeal to people with varying travel interests and experience. They can each be appropriate in specific social, economic and organisational circumstances, or inappropriate in other destinations.

The significance of these points is developed in the next two chapters. Chapter 3 investigates the perspectives of destination residents and managers on tourists' activities. Chapter 4 reviews destination marketing decisions, arguing that effective destination marketing requires not only that managers understand how and why people make their choice of destination, but pay attention to the aspects of their visit that prove satisfying.

Further reading

Bell, G. (1907) *The Desert and the Sown*, republished by Virago Press, London, 1985.

Chisnall, P. M. (1985) *Marketing, A Behavioural Analysis*, London: McGraw-Hill.

MacCannell, D. (1992) *Empty Meeting Grounds*, London: Routledge.

Pearce, P. L. (1988) *The Ulysses Factor, Evaluating Visitors in Tourist Settings*, New York: Springer Verlag.

Urry, J. (1990) *The Tourist Gaze, Leisure and Travel in Contemporary Society*, London: Sage, London.

Suggested exercises

1 Interview a convenient sample of people to investigate how they selected their most recent holiday destination. Compare your findings to the decision tree analysis.

2 Interview two different 'types' of tourist visiting a city for a long weekend, and draw up time budgets of their activities.

3 Describe how you introduced a family visitor to features of your home area.

4 Contrast your experiences of visiting areas new to you:

- in the company of a group of friends (for example a sports team);
- as a customer on an organised excursion;
- by yourself.

5 Account for the popularity of 'medieval' banquets and jousting tournaments.

3
The effects of tourism

Introduction

This chapter investigates the beneficial and harmful effects on destination areas which result from tourism development and tourists' activities. The numbers and types of its visitors, and its own morphology (the destination's geographical, social and ecological characteristics) affect its ability to absorb tourism activity. The impacts of a coach party sightseeing in a small historic town will be different from the same degree of tourist activity in a capital city. A thousand people spending a week at an established beach resort are unlikely to cause the same degree of concern as a thousand people hiking the paths of a Welsh mountainside at lambing time. The greater the economic and social diversity of the destination, and the more facilities it has for visitors, the more easily it will accommodate additional tourists, or new forms of tourism. The destination area's land forms and ecology, its economic and social structure and political organisation, determine the form and structure within which tourist activity produces specific local results.

As the general destination systems model (Figure 1.7) showed, tourist activity results in different outcomes for the stakeholders in an area, its residents, investors and employees. Those entrepreneurs catering to tourists' needs may prosper, new leisure amenities may be built to the benefit of residents as well as visitors, new jobs may be provided, resulting in further increases in economic activity, and beauty areas or endangered species may gain from the increased protection which tourists' interest causes. On the other hand, retail and residential property values may be forced up, to the detriment of existing businesses and residents, beaches and other areas may be fenced off, 'improved', and access limited to those able to pay for entry. In summary, introducing or expanding tourism in any destination results in changes.

Social carrying capacity

Tourism is a specialised form of leisure. Whereas most leisure activities take place in familiar surroundings, near one's home and amongst friends, tourism entails a temporary break from routine, undertaken in relatively unfamiliar settings, in the company of people who are mainly strangers. Thus, tourism represents 'counter routine' in Jost Krippendorf's (1987) memorable phrase. He, and others (notably Kelly, 1990) have pointed out that as well as providing personal freedom and opportunities for self expression, leisure is also about social interaction. Often, tourists leave behind them many of the social norms which regulate their activity at home or at work, and feel relatively free to indulge in a relaxed dress code, loose sexual morals or heavy drinking and over eating. Residents in many destinations have therefore come to regard hedonistic behaviour as typical of tourists. This presents particularly acute problems when previously remote areas experience a high level of tourism activity. Pi-Sunyer discussed Cap Lloc in the 1960s.

> Virtually every tourist proclaims his alienness through dress, speech and manners . . . the tourist enjoyed leisure at the very moment when the local inhabitants had to work hardest. Furthermore . . . somatic differences (blond hair, blue eyes, and a light complexion) spelled money. Finally, most tourists are city people, again a very different world.
>
> (Pi-Sunyer, 1989)

Picard has illustrated the situation in Bali.

> Visitors arrive (in Bali) as individuals with a high standard of living who are more or less frustrated in their own culture and then attempt to idealise a civilisation they can only appreciate superficially, identifying it with a lost civilisation they hope to see preserved. . . . The hosts, on the other hand, only see the exterior trappings of a foreign

way of life and are tempted to think of the countries from which the tourists have come as a sort of promised land they must make all effort to emulate.

(Pickard, 1991)

Ryan (1991) has identified a set of factors which lead to the emergence of a 'tourist culture', amongst the large number of temporary visitors and seasonal workers in destination areas. Neither group has a long-term commitment to the area, and both have an unusual daily pattern of activities: tourists can arrive at any time of the day or night, and their unconstrained spending makes it profitable to provide many services on a 24-hour basis throughout the peak season.

A typical pattern in the development of tourism is that a region experiences a gradual increase in the number of visitors, until some crisis level is reached after which the character of the area alters fundamentally, so that its amenities and infrastructure reflect the needs of tourists rather than residents. Doxey (1976) proposed the 'Iridex', a model cataloguing the increasing irritation of residents as the impact of visitor numbers increases. In the early stages of an isolated, self-sufficient and traditional community, the arrival of occasional visitors is flattering and they are welcomed. Doxey called this the *'euphoric stage'*, when the pleasure of welcoming visitors is real.

As the number of visitors increases, residents' euphoria may be replaced by *'apathy'*, when their willingness to interact with visitors is much less evident, and then by irritation. The 'irritation stage' of the Iridex model results from the concessions which have to be made to the increasing flow of temporary visitors in the form of specialised amenities and the competition for resources which drives up prices, but also, residents are offended that their visitors exhibit little real interest in local customs. Apathy and irritation are exacerbated because tourists are visibly different in their dress, they have extensive free time, they spend money freely and consequently become the targets of exploitative or even *antagonistic* behaviour by some locals. The final stage of Doxey's Iridex model recognises that sheer pressure of visitor numbers can *damage* what first drew them to an area, for example its traditional architecture, the traditional values of its residents, or even its lack of modern amenities such as fax or television.

There is another problem linked to this discussion. In the increasingly competitive marketplace for visitors, managers stake their claim for potential clients by 'positioning' their destination. The next chapter will show that this entails a systematic assessment of the area's unique or strongest characteristics, and its promotion through evocative marketing communications. The focus in text and imagery is often on traditional dress and craft skills, or the scenery and styles of building which, it is felt, typify the area and will entice tourists to visit it. The result of this approach is that many visitors expect to see a romanticised society leading a colourful, simple life in verdant, sanitised settings. Figure 3.1 contrasts the different attitudes of tourists and residents, summarising the foregoing discussion. The outcomes may be beneficial both for residents and visitors, but the model identifies potential sources of conflict.

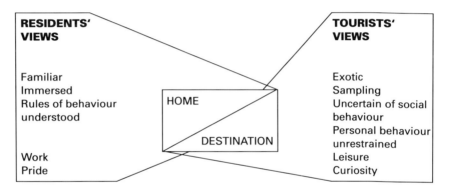

Figure 3.1 Contrasts between tourists' and residents' attitudes to a destination

Contemporary governments and destination administrators often express a wish to develop 'sustainable' forms of tourism, and their concern can be seen as a response to the extreme stage of the Iridex, in which they adopt policies intended to refocus on the beneficial aspects of tourism for the destination. The challenge in setting appropriate levels of tourist activities in a particular area is to decide what to measure, and how to do so. Defert has developed a Tourist Function Index (Defert, 1967, cited in Smith, 1989) to measure tourism intensity. This approach compares the number of tourists to the resident population, based on a count of bed spaces. However, one criticism is that various forms of accommodation attract different tourists on the basis of cost, comfort and amenities. That is, bed spaces are non-homogenous in nature, and it has already been pointed out that the specific impacts

of tourists depends on their activities and interests. A further methodological limitation is that many visitors do not use commercial bed
spaces, either because they stay with friends and relatives, or because
they are day visitors, perhaps coming in from paid temporary
accommodation outside the destination's boundaries. For example,
many of Canterbury's visitors are tourists from America or elsewhere,
who base their stay in London because of the range of cultural and
other tourist facilities it provides, but take a day trip to Canterbury,
usually by coach.

As Ziffer (1989) has pointed out, the social and environmental effects
of tourism are exacerbated in destinations located in areas which had
remained unmodernised until tourism led to their development. Walle
(1993) has examined the cultural conservation movement which aims
to help traditional populations practise self-determinism and deal
effectively with the world outside, the mainstream culture from which
tourists usually come. He argues that traditional people tend to be
regarded as 'quaint vestigial remains, surviving in the cocoon of hinter-
land retreats where the dominant culture has not yet entrenched itself'.
The temptation is for governments and the tourist industry to regard
them as a tourist resource, and tourists are conditioned to adopt this
perspective too, by the way their crafts and traditions are presented in
publicity material, and in themed interpretations. Walle advocates that
tourism has a role in preserving the dignity of people and the viability
of their cultural tradition as the society is transformed. Case study F
examines these and related issues in developing tourism in the Manu
National Park.

Case study F

Tourism in the Manu

Manu is one of three jungle reserves in the Madre de Dios area
of Peru. Covering 1.8 million hectares on the Eastern slopes of
the Andes, the parkland rises from an altitude of 365 metres to
4,020 metres, and is one of the most isolated and least colonised
of Amazonia's primary forests. Its significance is that the area has
the world's greatest diversity of animals, including jaguars, ocelots,
tapirs, 28 species of parrot, condors and eagles, boa and Andean

---

Case study F *(continued)*

snakes, and over 5,000 kinds of flowering plants, and it is believed that many other species remain to be studied. Manu park was established in 1973 to preserve the area's natural and cultural heritage for the benefit of present and future generations. In 1977 UNESCO accepted a proposal from the government of Peru to establish the Manu Biosphere Reserve, and in 1978 Manu was added to the World Heritage List.

The river basins are the homeland of a variety of indigenous groups still practising their traditional way of life. The peoples living in the Park are autonomous, and continue with their traditional means of food production, medicine and social customs. Their understanding of the Amazonian environment and their ability to survive without damaging it, is respected by the Peruvian authorities.

The journey to Manu from Cusco by plane, bus and river boat is described by the Peruvian Tourist Board as 'difficult' and visitors require a permit for entry to the park. The only accommodation within the park is Manu Lodge. This was built in 1987, without felling any mature trees, out of logs salvaged from the river and bought from locals. In the last year for which figures are available (1989) Manu lodge contributed approximately 25 per cent of the park's operating budget. Half of this came from a contribution of 5 per cent of the lodge's gross income, and half resulted from the park fees paid by lodge clients. Clients are guided in the forest by resident biologists whose primary function is long-term research into the ecology of the region, and some of the indigenous people demonstrate their work and craft skills to visitors. The lodge has acquired VHF radio equipment, both as a safety precaution for the boats it operates, and so that the indigenous jungle guides can report animal sightings to the benefit of guests setting out on escorted walks or river trips.

The owner of Manu Lodge, Boris Gomez Luna (who also operates Manu Nature Tours) explained his dedication to the preservation of the area's unique natural resources, and their enjoyment by visitors.

Case study F *(continued)*

When I recall my first experience in Manu, I always remember the total freedom, the complete serenity, the perfect balance. . . . I also remember the heat, the downpours, the long hours on the back of an old lumber truck. . . . The trails served for a group of tourists to visit Manu. The experience could not be called successful, the Manu was still too primitive, too rough for normal people. At that time, Manu was only for crazy explorers and hard scientists. . . . I had to develop the infrastructure and the logistics to bring in supplies. . . . In order to succeed in an environment like Manu, you need the best technology you can afford for communications and transport. . . . We put together a slide show and talked to radio stations, newspapers, politicians and entrepreneurs to establish the Conservation Association for the Rain forest. The local tourist businesses still depend on us for advertising and business.

We do not throw refuse on the water, we use percolation pits for sewage and showers, and oxidation pits for tin, paper and bio degradable material. We take out of the park all plastic, glass and aluminium.

My idea for expansion is a series of lodges distributed along the different habitats of the Manu. This way, instead of having 90 people packed in one place, we will have three times more, but distributed amongst many lodges. . . . I would prefer that other people develop some of the projects so that the effect multiplies, and encourages locals to see their place as valuable. . . . We are hoping to get scientific and financial assistance to develop a lodge in the Manu Cloud Forest. We would like to make flora and fauna inventories, and develop educational projects in ecology . . . as part of a plan to use the reserve. Manu Lodge has begun to purchase food such as manioc, bananas and brazil nuts from the surrounding community, and also sells handicrafts made by the Piro Indians, all profits being passed on to them. Beside the mountain biking, river running, horse riding and trekking that can lure tourists, we are also thinking of orchids and ornamental plants as a way to develop the economy of the area.

Case study F *(continued)*

Sources: InfoPeru, and the Manu Lodge newsletter, various editions, and personal communications from Glyn Lovell Tourism Services.

Suggested exercise

Interview the manager of a local heritage or ecological site, and summarise the views expressed in the form of an article for publication in either the travel or the general features section of an appropriate national newspaper.

An increase in tourism activity may present destination managers with several related problems. Residents become progressively more irritated with visitors, tourists seem less interested in the local culture, preferring to see commercialised, stylised versions and businesses begin to lose their local flavour, stocking a bland range of international brands

Table 3.1 Social policy responses to support tourism development

---

Tourism awareness programmes
to broadcast the benefits of tourism to the local community, emphasising its importance in terms of income and employment, or explaining that tourism stimulates the provision of amenities and infrastructure for everyone

Explain local values to outsiders
inform tourists (or the organisations which arrange their visits or invest in facilities for tourists) what residents expect of them

Explain to residents what people visiting the region want
in terms of opportunities to see the everyday life of the community

Explain the standards of service tourists expect
to managers of hotels, restaurants, shops and their staff, or to taxi drivers, the police, customs and other officials

Public awards for outstanding service
both by tourism employees and members of the general community whom tourists praise

---

which are more familiar to tourists than the locally produced variants. The Hawaii Visitor Bureau dealt with this in an advertisement directed to Island businesses.

> Keep it Hawaii. . . . Hula is good for business. . . . Your business can add to the magic of Hawaii by sharing examples of our heritage and traditions. Hawaiian music, a hula demonstration, or the simple gift of a flower can create lasting memories for visitors. Better still, your efforts give back to the community by helping preserve the true essence of Hawaii. . . .

> (cited in Buck, 1993)

Table 3.1 outlines five social policy responses which have particular relevance for destinations coping with an increase in tourism, while case study G discusses some of the social factors considered in the Tourism Development Plan for Western Samoa.

Case study G

Cultural considerations in tourism planning for Western Samoa

The 6th Development Plan (1988–90) identified the factors constraining economic growth in Western Samoa as the nation's geographic isolation, its small domestic market, its limited resource endowment, its vulnerability to international trade conditions, the subsistence-based production system and outward migration. Ethnic Samoans living abroad constitute a large proportion of tourists, returning to visit friends and relatives, and to conduct business. Holiday traffic accounts for about one-third of visitor arrivals, which have increased by less than 3 per cent per annum between 1984 and 1990. The factors constraining holiday traffic include the lack of investment in hotels and the limited nature of Western Samoa's tourist product. Western Samoa's relatively large trade deficit has been financed by foreign remittances and aid, and from tourism earnings.

Since the mid-1980s a series of reports have recommended that Western Samoa should adopt the goal of moderate tourism development, arguing that tourism helps to preserve the country's

Case study G *(continued)*

heritage and protect its natural environment. However, action was not specified in detail, and a new long-term plan was published in 1992, based on field work by the Tourism Council of the South Pacific, evaluation of all previous reports, and consultation with government officials. The draft had been prepared for submission to the Cabinet when a tropical cyclone severely damaged Western Samoa in December 1991, a further revision to the plan took into account the effects of the cyclone on the tourism sector.

There are nine islands in Western Samoa; two, Upolu and Savai'i, account for 96 per cent of the land area, and receive most of the tourists. Both islands are about 72 km long, they are both mountainous and have rich tropical rainforest with fern, orchids, bats, butterflies, and the tooth-billed pigeon, the only extant relative of the dodo. The 1986 census recorded a population of 157,000, 80 per cent living in rural villages, with 59 per cent of the economically active population categorised as 'working primarily to grow, gather, or catch food to eat' and 40 per cent 'to earn money' of whom 76 per cent are female, compared to 22 per cent of workers in the traditional subsistence sector. The Asian Development Bank report commented that 'Although unemployment as such seems virtually non existent, there appears to be widespread underemployment, particularly (amongst those engaged primarily to gather food to eat).

Against this background, tourism offers employment opportunities in hotels, restaurants, tour transport companies, souvenir shops, information services, and indirectly in sectors supplying inputs to tourism organisations. However, in advocating tourism, the plan points out that some aspects of traditional Western Samoan culture must be taken into consideration when developing and managing the tourism industry.

1 Traditional land tenure

All members of an extended family have rights of access and use to their land in perpetuity. The family chief is its custodian, and

Case study G *(continued)*

the land, together with the family, establishes an individual's identity, but land boundaries are informal. The construction of virtually all tourism facilities involves the demarcation of land and its appropriation to uses other than for subsistence agriculture. The lack of fixed boundaries means that ownership is unclear, and traditional owners tend to overestimate its value to developers. Their expectations of high sales values are based on their perception of tourists as wealthy, and enjoying expensive facilities. Two suggestions were made to counteract this problem:

1 One proposal is a leaflet to explain the land tenure system to developers, and the processes required to secure a piece of land for any tourism project. This would be matched by education of land-owning groups through village councils.
2 The second proposal is an alternative to financial compensation for land given to tourism projects, encouraging land-owning groups to become share-holding partners and to participate in the industry.

2 The villages

Villages throughout Western Samoa are interested in hosting tourists. The impetus comes from individual entrepreneurial responses to the interest of visitors in their traditional ways of life. In the mid-1990s, the limited number of visitors is easily absorbed, but increasing numbers pose a threat to work patterns, and the rhythm of social activities. Traditionally, Samoan villagers have welcomed visits from their neighbours, but the relationships and behaviours of host and guest are clear and well understood. However, tourists do not behave as Samoans expect, and the risk is that village hospitality will be abused resulting in the curtailment of these developments.

The Plan recommends that visitors should be briefed about appropriate behaviour in a non-cash society, while village councils and women's committees should also be educated about appropriate forms of hospitality in the context of tourism.

Case study G *(continued)*

Sources: Western Samoa Tourism Development Plan, 1992–2001, and interviews with Samoan tourism officials and managers.

Suggested exercise

Draft a letter from the developer to residents of a small village in Sussex informing them that a major theme park will be constructed nearby.

Tourists who visit an area on a regular basis often form an emotional attachment to it, and buy property in the area, either as a holiday home, or for their retirement. This stimulates the area's economy by the increased building activity and the extra demand for goods and services when the second-home owners (or their guests) are resident. However, second-home ownership can cause great friction with the area's traditional residents for reasons indicated in Figure 3.2. A study of second homes owned on Skye found that 42 per cent were used less than five weeks of the year, that only 46 per cent had been inherited, that 65 per cent of owners lived in Edinburgh, Glasgow or London, and that 61 per cent of them intended to retire to the island. Islanders complained that city dwellers were buying up their houses, there were too many old people on the island, locals could not afford the houses and many were empty for most of the year, and their essential services were reduced. Similar problems have been reported from Cornwall, Wales and attractive areas in many other countries.

In a presentation to the Tourism Society in 1993, Fairs, Director of Langdale Leisure Ltd gave a rationale for timeshare development in the Lake District. He argued that time share owners obtain most of the benefits sought from second-property purchase, without facing the problems of maintenance and heating during the winter, or the potential for vandalism during the period they are empty. The traditional community also benefits because the timeshare property is staffed year-round, and provides restaurant and meeting amenities for the area.

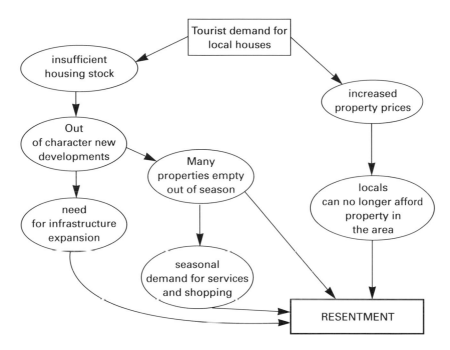

Figure 3.2 Consequences of second-home ownership

But the greatest advantages of timeshared property is that building pressure on the countryside is limited, while many tourists can enjoy residential status in an attractive region.

The economic impacts of tourism

Governments often encourage tourism. The reasons for their enthusiasm vary, ranging from the lack of any viable alternative when an existing industrial or primary sector declines, or because jobs in the tourism sector are relatively quick and cheap to create, while the influx of affluent visitors stimulates the general economic development of the region, bringing in convertible currency.

As tourist arrivals increase, the various supplies and services needed by hotels, catering and transport operators, and other facilities mean that tourism becomes a key element in the business environment for existing companies. The construction industry benefits from hotel and infrastructure projects, dairies, market gardeners and fruit farmers have new customers, garages are required to supply and service fleets of delivery vehicles and rental cars. Tourism also offers a variety of entry points to the workforce, both for skilled and first-time employees. As case study H on Tibet indicates, the increased spending power in the area, and the presence of people with varied interests also results in an environment conducive to starting many types of small business.

Case study H

Tourism employment in Tibet

In the mid-1980s Tibet's borders were opened to international tourists for the first time. The country had been isolated from outside influence for several centuries, but had been subjected to the harsh rule of Chinese administrators for two decades. The result was that Tibet's medieval theocracy had been undermined and many of its great temples and traditions had been destroyed or severely damaged. However, the allure of this remote, virtually medieval country proved attractive to tourists. This case study considers some of the difficulties faced by its tourism managers, and the opportunities which tourism presented to Tibetans.

The managers of the Lhasa Hotel, Tibet's flagship hotel, explained how they had brought it up to the standards of the Holiday Inn group which had taken on the management contract. Their first priority had been 'to minimise shouting by the guests', as their company had been brought in when service standards were poor. The Chinese 'iron rice bowl' policy of permanent employment had made it very hard to sack incompetent or under performing staff: 98 per cent of the people working in the Lhasa Hotel had to be retained by the new management. The turn-around in service standards was based on training, concentrating on language skills, especially English, and service skills, teaching local girls the appropriate dress for restaurant service, and emphasising personal cleanliness as service was a totally new concept to Tibetans.

It was not customary for young Tibetan ladies to clean their finger nails, and in the winter they objected to covering their

Case study H *(continued)*

newly acquired jeans with the uniforms we issued, so we had to compromise by getting them to roll the legs up.

Interviews with hotel managers

Jobs in the hotel were regarded as prestigious because of the opportunities to meet Westerners. Pay was good by local standards, and uniquely in Tibet, wages were supplemented by incentive schemes and employee service recognition programmes. The dormitory was said to be the only one in Lhasa to provide central heating in the winter, and staff received three meals a day plus free medical care. Staff from other hotels were also attracted to work in the Lhasa Hotel by the greater work discipline and the training opportunities offered. In summer 1987 the compliment was 650 staff recruited locally, with 15 managers from Hong Kong, 28 from Beijing and 5 from overseas.

Tibetans responded quickly to the opportunities for small enterprise offered by tourist spending power. Tibetan businessmen began to build small hotels aimed at backpackers, and to establish travel agencies, sometimes in collaboration with foreign investors. Milk, fruit and vegetables were supplied to the hotels by local producers, and the authorities encouraged this diversification from the traditional staple diet as a means of improving local health, and because they hoped for a surplus to export to other parts of China.

Roadside stalls had begun to sell a limited range of souvenirs such as sweatshirts featuring the Potala and other notable Tibetan attractions. In the absence of a network of town buses, transport was provided by farmers, and tourists could often be seen riding in their unsprung tractor-trailer combinations to outlying temples, or around the town. The revenue from these activities was said to exceed earnings from agricultural efforts, and the scale of diverted resources cast some doubt on the feasibility of meeting local agricultural production targets.

Source: Laws (1991, modified).

Case study H *(continued)*

Suggested exercise

Contrast the opportunities for tourism employment and enterprise in a small city and a beach resort.

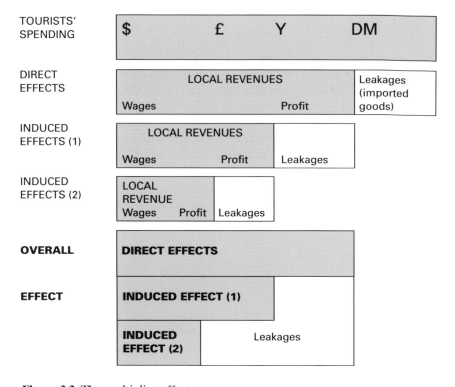

Figure 3.3 The multiplier effect

The benefit of spending by tourists spreads through many sectors of the community, and can be traced through the multiplier effect. This method measures the direct spending power of visitors, and calculates how their initial spending round (and what it implies in employment) is amplified as the resident population subsequently spends some of the extra revenue earned as profit or income, thereby further stimulating economic activity. Figure 3.3 illustrates the potency of the multiplier effect, showing that the full benefit of the initial tourist spending is dissipated by two factors:

1 Tourists buy some imported goods with the result that the benefit leaks away from the destination community.
2 Some of the initial earnings are saved rather than spent.

Similarly, the jobs which are created to provide services directly to tourists are augmented as other people are employed indirectly, in the firms which provide supplementary services such as cleaning and maintenance to hotels, and car hire firms. In turn, the additional spending power which results induces a third set of jobs providing for the needs of these employees.

The employment potential of tourism compared with other industries has been criticised on several grounds:

● that much employment is seasonal;
● the local population is often too small (or unwilling) to fill the vacancies;
● in many areas there are insufficient workers with specific technical and managerial skills;
● outsiders are attracted in by high wages and the opportunity to live and work in pleasant or exotic surroundings.

The result is an inflow of seasonal employees who have a higher degree of contact with visitors than typical residents. Thus, the immigrant workers get much of the initial employment benefit. A further problem is that tourism employment may attract workers away from other sectors because of the opportunities it offers to meet outsiders, to learn new skills or to earn high commissions. Other criticisms of tourism's employment have been directed at the sector in developed countries. These relate to its limited career potential, the unsocial hours often required, and the high proportion of low-paid, seasonal and temporary jobs which are normally filled by women, or by students in the peak season. To the extent that poor working conditions demoralise or disenchant staff serving in tourism organisations, the risk is that low service standards may result.

Although tourism can create many economic benefits for a destination, there are also costs associated with its development. A destination with a particular level of infrastructure, pool of labour and amenities for tourism can accommodate a finite number of visitors in a given period. Beyond this level, its current economic carrying capacity is inadequate and one of two consequences will result. Without additional facilities or new workers, visitors will judge the local standards inadequate, and go elsewhere. The alternative is to improve the infrastructure, invest in the tourism sector and encourage people to move into the area to fill the employment vacancies. This represents a discontinuity in the development of the area, and while the results may be beneficial, the point is that a significant change in the area has been caused by tourism.

Misra (1993) has discussed the Indian Government's plans for a 'culturally and environmentally appropriate' park as a buffer zone around one of its major tourist attractions, the Taj Mahal. The purpose is to preserve the Taj Mahal from development and pollution, and to provide an appropriate setting for the Taj, thus making it more enjoyable to visit, both for tourists and residents. A court judgement has ordered the closure of 2,200 factories which were considered a threat to the monument and a residential area is planned for local craftsmen, many of whose ancestors built the monument. They will be encouraged to continue their crafts within a traditional ambience, to the interest of visitors who will form a market for their output.

The development of a major tourism sector imposes a variety of costs on the host community, as additional amenities and infrastructure improvements are required to change an area into a competitive destination. Table 3.2 summarises the costs of infrastructure development required to service resort developments proposed on the Big Island of Hawaii.

Given its significance in leading the general development of an area, tourism sometimes claims priority over other users for resources. Tourism has been encouraged in China to promote the economy, but conflicts have been identified with other sectors. 'Modern hotels are a giant consumer of energy. . . . To ensure the supply of electricity and water to the international hotels, energy departments frequently have to switch off supplies to factories, ignoring their urgent appeals' (Ma Ruilin, 1992). Other economic problems arise from operating tourism services. Murphy (1985) has cited Heeley's study of the costs

Table 3.2 Costs of infrastructure development in West Hawaii

	Infrastructure estimates $ million
Airport expansion	156
Major road improvement	106
Harbours	36
Hospitals	12
Library	14
Police and emergency services	28
Schools	72
Water supply	47
Sewage	25
Drainage	55
Solid waste	5
Recreation and parks	65
Total public infrastructure improvements (estimated):	$622 million

Source: West Hawaii Plan (Appendix C).

incurred in one area for fire support to local tourism businesses. Of 4,023 total calls during the period studied, 92 were to tourism enterprises. Since the fire service cost £2,767,000 to run, a simple calculation showed that the community had incurred a 'tourism fire cost' of £63,300.

The environmental consequences of tourism

Tourism, like any other large scale human activity, can have adverse consequences for the land, vegetation and wildlife in the areas where it occurs. One of the ironies of modern society has been the shift of populations to urban centres, coinciding with greatly improved mobility which has enabled large numbers of people to leave the cities for recreation in rural, mountainous or seaside areas. They are attracted by the more tranquil pace of life away from the cities, and by the opportunity to observe wildlife in its natural habitat, or to experience the thrill of adventure in remote or dangerous environments. The environmental consequences of tourist activity are often difficult to isolate from other developments resulting from demographic, technological, or agricultural changes. Extreme environments such as the polar regions provide a laboratory within which tourism issues are relatively easy to isolate for identification and study, consequently case study I examines the effects of tourism in Antarctica.

Case study I

Environmental consequences of tourism in Antarctica

Noble Caledonian advertised a seventeen-day fly-cruise to Antarctica, to take place in January 1995. This cruise will be accompanied by Sir Ranulph Fiennes, an experienced explorer, and by a team of naturalists. After a flight to Santiago and a charter flight to Ushuaia in Southern Argentina, clients will join a custom-built exploration vessel accommodating 90 passengers for a two-day cruise during which albatross and whales will probably be sighted. A further five days will then be spent cruising the waters off the Antarctica Peninsula, where the programme includes viewing wildlife and the coastal scenery. The company emphasise the benefits of travelling in a small vessel:

> We will have the opportunity to spend many hours ashore, and although the itinerary is by necessity flexible we will aim to make only one visit to a base, as to us Antarctica is 'nature' and not the less attractive human enterprises. . . .
>
> With a small party aboard, the cruise is like a mini expedition in itself, akin to having one's own yacht for Polar exploration. . . . Such limited numbers do not infringe upon the fragile environment. . . . After all, once the passengers begin to outnumber the penguins the very appeal of Antarctica will be lost.

The return journey to Britain includes a three-night stay in Santiago, at prices ranging from £4,498 to £7,686 depending on the grade of cabin booked.

Antarctica has only recently been opened to tourist visits, although overflights were popular in the 1970s, and tourism remains at a low level of development, as Table 3.3 indicates. However, in 1992, a total of 27,821 tourists visited the continent, and Chile had established the first hotel in Antarctica.

Until 1990, the impact of visitors was relatively easy to control, as two (American) companies dominated tourism to Antarctica, but the growth in tourism arrivals has been paralleled by a proliferation of tour operators. The revenue from commercial tourism

Case study I *(continued)*

Table 3.3 Tourist arrivals in Antarctica

	Mode of travel		
	Sea	*Air*	*Total*
1980	–	–	855
1982	719	2	721
1991	6,313	178	6,491
1992	26,224	1,597	27,821

Source: Enzenbacher, 1993.

has the potential to subsidise government operations in Antarctica, and to justify claims to territory there, but the presence of tourists disrupts scientific programmes, and is causing concern in a continent where 60 per cent of the terrestrial and 70 per cent of marine life is endemic.

Beck (1994) regards tourism as 'the key current issue confronting the Antarctic Treaty Parties'. He states that the 1991 Protocol on Environmental Protection and Annexes to the Antarctic Treaty which 'apply to tourist and non governmental activities in Antarctica' has not been formally ratified, and countries with access to the region have differing attitudes. One of the problems in Antarctica is that the surface is extremely fragile, it is said that a footprint in the moss is still visible after a decade. Most visitors are attracted by the area's specialised ecology and wildlife, and a visit to Antarctica is expensive. The inevitable consequence is that tourists will put pressure on their guides and destination managers to show them the animals and birds of Antarctica, and as their numbers increase, so does the likelihood of damage. These concerns have led to pressure for a tour operator policy. 'A better understanding of tourism impacts would aid the formulation of a comprehensive tourism policy to be agreed within the Antarctic Treaty System' (Hall and McArthur, 1993). One approach is to limit the number of visitors, and they report that New Zealand set a quota of 500 visitors to

Case study I *(continued)*

the Campbell and Auckland Isles in 1991. This included 'all existing human activities other than those directly involved in scientific research and the normal operations of government bases.' Tourists coming via New Zealand are charged a levy of NZ$100 each, this has financed the construction of a one kilometre boardwalk so that tourists can view an albatross colony without harming the surface.

The majority of tourists come to Antarctica on cruises from South America or New Zealand which, although they last up to a month, give only a few hours ashore, but the potential for environmental damage is real. Ships have been observed discharging sewage tanks or cleaning their fuel bunkers, and kitchen waste washes ashore in some parts of Antarctica, and cruises visit the area in the summer, which is the peak breeding season.

Sources: based on articles cited, and interviews with naturalists.

Suggested exercise

Justify either the right of tour operators to organise visits to Antarctica, or the grounds for excluding non-scientific visitors from the region.

In contrast to the discussion of Antarctic tourism, the vast majority of tourism activity takes place in destinations where human populations have established a balance with the environment they inhabit, but tourism brings into an area a much greater number of people than its resources traditionally sustained. Budowski (1976) investigated the relationship between conservation and tourism, and distinguished three characteristic cases.

1 In places where visitors have limited interest in the local ecology, conservation programmes are unlikely to persist.
2 In other places, tourists' insensitive use of an area may bring them into conflict with conservationists.

3 The most positive situation occurs when tourists visit and enjoy the natural attributes of an area, resulting in a supportive relationship between conservation and tourism, however, Budowski cautioned that this symbiotic relationship is rare.

Pigram has addressed the problem of identifying what level of tourism is acceptable in a given environment, suggesting that the critical issue is the ability of natural resources to regenerate. This level has to be evaluated in the particular ecology of each location, but three factors are crucial.

1 *Uniqueness* – the differentiation of a given natural element in a region;
2 *Fragility* – its ability to regenerate and resist tourism effects;
3 *Naturalness* – how far the area has been altered from its natural state.

(Pigram, 1990)

A study of the dive industry in Hawaii found that participants had increased from 474,000 in 1975, to about 2 million in 1988. Tabata (1992) distinguished between 'hard-core divers' who choose a destination because of the challenge of its diving conditions, or because of the diversity of its flora and fauna, and 'tourist divers' who include scuba diving as a part of their holiday. Both hard-core and tourist divers are attracted to Hawaii by its reefs, wrecks, shells, caves, with good water quality, safe, easy access to the sites, and the diversity of marine life. Tourism to Hawaii's resorts has resulted in pressures on the marine environment caused by water pollution, fresh water run off, litter, and siltation, thus prejudicing the future of the dive industry. However, diving also causes damage, through collecting specimens, and boats dragging their anchors through coral.

This form of special interest tourism has an organised structure, the 47 dive shops which Tabata studied sold a quarter of a million dives worth $19.8 million, generating 7.4 per cent of Hawaii's ocean recreation revenues in 1986. 54,000 were introductory dives, 68,000 certified, and 128,000 snorkelling. Of the 196 dive sites, 70 were used most frequently because of fast access.

The dive operator is an intermediary decision maker between the resource and the user; the operator generally decides what sites will be visited by their customers . . . will know what dive site features would be attractive and satisfying to customers. Therefore it is assumed that the operators' preferences generally reflect the desires and expectations of their customers.

(Tabata, 1992)

He pointed out that better understanding of why operators (and their clients) favour certain sites will help Hawaii's resource managers and tourism development agencies to provide a range of diving opportunities that will attract dive travellers and minimise adverse impacts by dispersing diving to new areas.

Alternative forms of tourism-seeking symbiosis

Attention has already been drawn to the potentially adverse effects on destinations of increasing the scale of tourism activity. It has been argued that the arrival of a few travellers has little impact on the traditional life and organisation of communities. At some point in the development of a destination, the regular arrival of increasing numbers of visitors has consequences which represent a discontinuity in the evolution of the area. However, it is not just a question of visitor numbers, the structural form of tourism activity locally is a mediating factor, as the previous chapter has indicated. In destinations where the predominant form of tourism is package holidays organised by tour operators based in the country from which visitors originate, several consequences can be observed, as indicated in Table 3.4.

The type of mass tourism described above tends to result in the commoditisation of tourist destinations. Destinations become substitutes for each other, tour operators' brochures emphasise general benefits such as beaches, and entertainment. In these circumstances, a client's choice between destinations reflects price advantages and convenience rather than the attributes of a specific place, its peoples and ecology.

Table 3.4 The consequences of packaged tourism for destinations

1 Tourists arrive in batches
2 They stay for regular periods
3 Their perceptions and expectations of the destination are influenced by the tour operator's promotional efforts
4 A routine is established by which each batch of visitors follows a rather similar programme of activities
5 Their involvement with the destination's culture and environment is largely determined by the tour operator

The commoditisation spiral is driven by four related factors:

1 Clients often have low loyalty to particular destinations.
2 Many tourists are keen to sample a variety of destinations.
3 Tour operators require consistent standards of facilities and service for their clients from every resort they do business with.
4 Tour operators are able to switch clients to alternative destinations for a variety of logistical or other reasons.

These standardising factors tend to conflict with Western society's growing interest in conservation and related issues, and has led to an increasingly vocal call for alternative forms of tourism which are more responsive to local community concerns, and which attract tourists who are more responsible in their behaviour.

Deciding the local future of tourism

The development of tourist activity is likely to alter the range and nature of public recreation as new amenities are provided or wilderness areas are equipped for increased visitor activity. Inevitably, this leads to management of the area, in the form of restrictions, regulations, and charges for use. Recreation, both for visitors and residents, becomes organised and structured, either in response to commercial opportunities, or in the interests of resource conservation.

Just as tourists differ from each other, so residents have differing experiences of, and different attitudes to, people visiting their area. Sheldon and Var (1984) found that the further residents lived from the tourist zone, the less likely they were to have negative opinions of tourism. They also pointed out that length of residence in the area would affect perceptions of tourism. Much tourism occurs in areas which are attractive, or which have benign climates such as the southern coasts of Spain, or Hawaii, and these areas also attract second-home owners or retired people. Um and Crompton (1987) have suggested that long-term residents may be less enthusiastic about visitors than newcomers to their community. Research is inconclusive, but the topic is a critical one given the goals stated for many tourism developments of enhancing residents' lifestyles, and the preceding discussion of tourists as a potential source of irritation to local residents.

The fundamental issue considered in this chapter is how to decide on the appropriate level of tourism activity for any area. The perspective from which one investigates this issue is relevant, as a study in Colorado

Table 3.5 Colorado residents' attitudes to tourism

Community group		Attitude towards tourism
Economic participation rate	*Extent of tourism development in area*	
Low	Low	High hopes from future tourism development
High	High	Favourable to further development
High	Low	No need for tourism development recognised
Low	High	Discourage further tourism development

Based on: Allen, *et al.*, 1993.

illustrates. Table 3.5 summarises the attitudes towards increases in tourism of four groups in the community.

This study reinforces the point made earlier in this book that the effects of tourism are unequally distributed amongst the resident population and other interest groups. The general tourist destination systems model (Figure 1.7), indicated that tourism has varied outcomes for each group involved, and this highlights the improbability of achieving a balance of advantages for all parties. Without a comprehensive assessment of all the effects, decisions about the future development of tourism are likely to reflect the interests of a region's most influential or vocal groups.

The people who experience the main impacts of tourism are those who live in the tourism destination areas, and ethical concerns suggest that their views and concerns should be considered in destination development. This entails establishing a clear framework to determine which questions need to be considered, and what factors should enter into policy decisions. Figure 3.4 illustrates some of the consequences for destinations of tourism, and Table 3.6 presents a summary of some of the key issues and the methods available to control visitor impacts.

Table 3.6 Contemporary objectives and methods in the control of tourist impacts

Community objectives

* Provide incentives for local ownership of tourist facilities
* Retain economic benefits of tourism locally
* Train residents to work in tourism at all levels
* Educate residents about tourism concepts, issues and benefits
* Maintain the authenticity of dance and handicrafts
* Ensure residents have access to tourist facilities
* Subsidise local or disadvantaged users

More responsible tourist behaviour

* Inform tourists about local customs
* Inform tourists about the local environment and ecology
* Encourage the types of tourists who will respect local traditions
* Control drugs, crime, and prostitution

Strategies for managing visitor impacts

Access
* Visa required
* Flight restrictions
* Hotel reservation required

Timed entry and stay
* Weekly charter flight arrivals
* Prebooking for entry to remote areas
* Onward (or return) ticket required

Pricing
* Separate currency for visitors
* Visitor services taxed (usually at a higher rate)
* Hotel or transport rates set high to exclude certain market segments, or low to encourage large numbers of visitors

Zoning
* Certain areas restricted to residents for privacy or security
* Tourists restricted (or encouraged to stay in) designated areas

Signposting
* Road signs to attract passing visitors
* Deliberate absence of signs to discourage casual visitors
* Interpretative labels to direct visitors around sites
* Notices restricting visitors to paths

Honeypotting
* Clustering amenities around entry points to discourage dispersal, especially in fragile environments
* Siting a new attraction away from resources already at or near capacity

Offer alternatives
* Brochures, advertisements and advertorial features highlighting the 'other' attractions of a place

a) Final approach to Athens

b) Tourist facilities at Sounion

Figure 3.4 Some consequences of tourism for destinations

c) Snowbird

d) Congestion in the mountains

Figure 3.4 (*continued*)

Conclusion

Effective responses to the issues discussed in this chapter depend on monitoring tourism's many impacts on a destination. Systematic investigation of the changing effects of tourism as it increases in an area will indicate the economic, social, and environmental benefits it creates, and can identify the various limits to tourism in the area.

Tourism is a relatively new industry, it is encouraging that business and government leaders are conscious of the harmful consequences that can result for destinations, and that they are seeking ways to mitigate these effects while ensuring that the benefits of tourism are spread more widely. But there are no universal solutions, what is needed is a framework within which the many effects of tourism for everyone in a destination area can be assessed. This chapter has demonstrated that the effects of tourism vary according to the type of visitors attracted to an area, and their activities while there. This point provides the link to the next two chapters, which examine the role played by marketing in the management of tourist destinations, and the role of destination planning.

Further reading

Baum, T. (ed.) (1993) *Human Resource Issues In International Tourism*, Oxford: Butterworth Heinemann.
Bull, A. (1991) *The Economics Of Travel And Tourism*, Melbourne: Pitman.
Edington, J. M. and Edington, M. A. (1990) *Ecology, Recreation and Tourism*, Cambridge: Cambridge University Press.
Martin, V. (ed.) (1988) *For The Conservation Of Earth*, Golden, CO: Fulcrum.
Mathieson, A. and Wall, G. (1982) *Tourism, Economic, Physical And Social Impacts*, Harlow: Longman.
Murphy, P. (1985) *Tourism, A Community Approach*, London: Methuen.
Smith, V. (ed.) (1989) *Hosts and Guests, The Anthropology of Tourism*, 2nd edn, Philadelphia: University of Pennsylvania Press.

Suggested exercises

1 Investigate the stock of accommodation available in a destination you are familiar with. Account for the relative importance of different types of accommodation: caravan parks, camp sites, guest houses, and hotels of various classifications.
2 Discuss the possible effects on the region's tourism of increasing one particular type of accommodation stock.
3 Draw up an indicative cost-benefit analysis of tourism in a small city or rural

area you are familiar with.

4 What should be monitored in the city's tourism information system, and how might the required data be collected?

5 Discuss the advantages and drawbacks of two or more alternative ways of limiting tourist use of specific areas. Contrast the perspectives of all stake-holders.

4
Marketing tourist destinations

Introduction

The key features of a market are the existence of a defined product or service which buyers are willing to pay for, and which sellers are eager to trade. Success for destination marketers depends on attracting sufficient temporary visitors to provide the economic demand needed by all the area's tourism businesses, and crucially, ensuring that visitors are satisfied with their experiences.

A tourist's choice of destination reflects the relative appeal to that individual of its attractions over those offered by competing places: the scenery, the beaches, the historic buildings, the quality and variety of shopping, the region's opportunities to relax or for sporting activities. Few of the organisations which provide services to tourists during their stay have the resources to promote themselves outside of their immediate area, and stimulating tourist markets is generally left to the major hotel groups and tour operators, or to the national airline or tourist organisation. Their main roles are therefore to create a favourable impression of their destination, thereby attracting tourists, and to determine how best to develop its amenities.

This chapter discusses the importance of marketing planning as a major management function for tourist destinations, before examining two key issues, the creation and promotion of appropriate destination images, and the network of business relationships through which destinations communicate with their customers.

Marketing planning processes for destinations

Each destination's managers have particular goals depending on its lifecycle stage, competition and other local priorities, but typically they include earning a given rate of profit from commercial operations, or they might be concerned with enhancing life quality measures for residents and visitors.

It is an axiom of modern management that planning is required to achieve those goals. Formal marketing planning is well documented, and has been adopted because it provides a rational, coherent framework for the many decisions that must be made to achieve organisational goals. Figure 4.1 illustrates the procedure for destination marketing planning. The traditional starting point for a marketing plan is *diagnosis*, that is the analysis of an organisation's current market performance, its consumers' behaviour and attitudes, and its competitors' strengths as well as other factors which could be significant, such as changes to relevant legislation, or new conditions in the economy. Diagnosis provides a detailed platform for *prognosis*, the forecasting of future trends for each of the market sectors of interest to the organisation, and specification of *actions* to be taken for each sector. Planning is an iterative process in the sense that the plan constantly evolves in the light of experience and evolving circumstances. The final, and key aspect of the planning process is a *control* system through which the implementation of the plan is monitored and results evaluated as a basis for further planning. Both the internal operation of an organisation, and circumstances in the market can lead to revision of planned targets.

However, it has been suggested in earlier chapters that destinations are characterised by a variety of business organisations, and fragmented co-ordination. Leppard and McDonald (1987) have argued that even in highly integrated and centralised businesses, the planning process and its outcomes reflect the realities of its internal politics and dynamics, a point which is highly relevant to the determination and implementation of destination policies, and is examined further in Chapter 5.

The situation facing a destination can be evaluated by a detailed consideration of the strengths and weaknesses of its current operations, and from scanning the various environmental influences for forthcoming threats or opportunities. The outcome is a formal SWOT analysis, such as Figure 4.2 which reviews the market for tourism in Kent just before the opening of the Channel Tunnel. The SWOT forms the context to

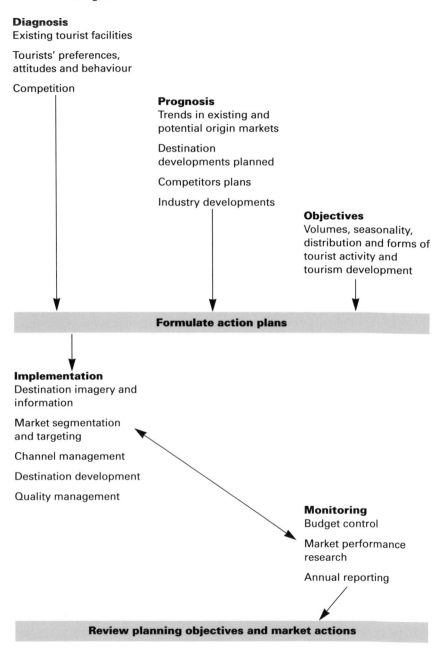

Diagnosis
Existing tourist facilities

Tourists' preferences,
attitudes and behaviour

Competition

Prognosis
Trends in existing and
potential origin markets

Destination
developments planned

Competitors plans

Industry developments

Objectives
Volumes, seasonality,
distribution and forms of
tourist activity and
tourism development

Formulate action plans

Implementation
Destination imagery and
information

Market segmentation
and targeting

Channel management

Destination development

Quality management

Monitoring
Budget control

Market performance
research

Annual reporting

Review planning objectives and market actions

Figure 4.1 Destination marketing planning

STRENGTHS	WEAKNESSES	ACTION
Heritage	Restricted opening	*Operation Offpeak*
Attractive coast	Pollution	*Blue Flag awards*
Shopping	Sunday closing	*Brighter Weekend campaign*
Free road network	Congestion	
OPPORTUNITIES	**THREATS**	
Kent as Britain's gateway to Europe	Visitors may transit Kent on improved road corridors	
High awareness of Tunnel	Tourist attractions being developed in northern France	

Figure 4.2 SWOT analysis of Kent prior to the opening of the Channel Tunnel, partly based on BTA, 1991

which the marketing plan relates, Case study J examines a marketing campaign developed by the South East England Tourist Board in response to these conditions.

Most destinations try to attract a variety of clients, for short breaks, business conferences, themed holidays and so on, and they offer a variety of services such as different levels of accommodation, sporting or cultural activities. The marketing plan deals with each major group in turn, identifying appropriate ways of attracting clients to each, considering ways to develop or adapt services, setting prices and creating promotional campaigns which it is hoped, will generate the visitors needed to achieve targets. The marketing plan sets subsidiary targets in terms of client numbers or value of sales for each of the destination's market segments and products, in many cases there will be a gap between present performance and the future sales, revenue or growth targets set in the plan. The marketing plan itself is largely concerned with the various steps needed to bridge those gaps during the term of its operation. The traditional 4Ps approach to marketing emphasises the tactical tools of *Promotion, Product, Pricing* and *Placing* (distribution), but destination marketers are also involved in a wide range of strategic and other functions (Laws, 1991).

Planning is also based on forecasts of anticipated future-period demand or altered competitive conditions rather than merely responding in an *ad hoc* fashion to events. Forecasts can be generated by projecting historic trends, anticipating major discontinuities such as new transport infrastructure, or by expert techniques such as the Delphic Oracle approach to forecasting. This is based on experts' judgements modified by increasing knowledge shared between them. The method consists of asking experts what they expect to happen, their answers are collated and fed back for further discussion. These steps are repeated, and an agreed view is reached (Moeller and Shaffer, 1987). The Chartered Institute of Marketing Travel Industry Group (in collaboration with the Tourism Society) conducts a bi-annual survey, asking their members to give their views about the future development of tourism, and a panel of senior managers then discusses the findings. Table 4.1 presents the responses to selected questions in 1991 and 1993.

Given the uncertainties of future events, and the margin for error in forecasting, a sound marketing plan will also specify interim performance measures by which progress may be judged. The actual results achieved at each stage act as feedback by which the later targets are modified in the light of experience, according to whether business has slipped or improved from the levels planned.

Another key role for marketing expertise is its contribution to long-run managerial decisions about what services the destination should offer in the future, and which markets to develop. Without the continuing refinement of existing tourism services the tourists a destination sells to at present are likely to be attracted away in the future by the new, improved or more sharply priced offers of its competitors. Development strategies can be categorised in terms of risk: the greater a destination's experience of dealing with a particular type of client such as young adventurers, or in selling particular types of holiday such as skiing, the more likely it is that a new service for these types of tourist will succeed. It is most risky to sell a new type of holiday to a segment of the market which the company has no experience of dealing with. Ansoff (1968) has argued that the decisions to be taken in regard to innovations fall into four broad risk categories.

1 *Continue to sell current services to existing customers* – the risk is that fewer clients will return each season.
2 *New services can be developed for existing clients* – there is no guarantee that they will indeed be attracted by the new style of holidays offered.

Table 4.1 Forecasts of changes in British tourism

By how much do you expect the overseas inclusive tour market to change over the next 3 years?

% change	1991 survey (%)	1993 survey (%)
−10	6	2
−5	29	10
no change	6	13
+5	39	54
+10	8	21
+15	3	2

What are the major areas of expansion in the overseas IT market in the next 3 years?

1991 forecasts	1993 forecasts
Low priced holidays	Youth market
Youth market	Low priced holidays
Seat only	Up market holidays
Up market	Seat only
Retirement	Retirement
Long-haul	Long-haul
Self-drive	Short breaks
Cruising	Activities
Special interest	Special interest
	Cruising
	Independent

How will Spain's share of the market have changed in 3 years?

	1991 survey (%)	1993 survey (%)
Increased	20	41
Decreased	80	56

How will America's share of the market have changed in 3 years?

	1991 survey (%)	1993 survey (%)
Increased	86	70
Decreased	14	27

How important an issue will the environment become for the tourism industry?

	1991 survey (%)	1993 survey (%)
Much more important	43	29
Slightly more	44	45
About the same	11	20
Slightly less important	2	4
Much less important	1	0

Source: CIMTIG/Tourism Society, in Laws, 1994.

3 *Existing services can be advertised to new clients* – the risk in this strategy is that inappropriate messages or media may be used, because these clients are unknown.
4 *New services can be developed for new clients* – this is the riskiest strategy because neither the operational aspects of the new facilities, nor the expectations of the new clients are known.

Segmenting the market for destinations

The technique of segmentation has been defined as: 'The process of dividing a potential market into distinct subsets of consumers, and selecting one or more segments as a target to be reached with a distinct marketing mix' (Wilkie, 1986). To be selected for management attention and action, any segment must have three characteristics:

1 It must be measurable.
2 It should be easy to reach through advertising and distribution systems.
3 It should offer a sustainable flow of business which will more than repay the costs of developing it.

(Woodside and Sherrill, 1977)

Effective market segmentation depends on research to identify the characteristics of the types of visitor who seek particular benefits from the destination. A typical method is to draw up a list of the primary and secondary destination attributes. People with relevant demographic characteristics are interviewed (or a focus group is held) to explore their interests, opinions and recreational preferences. Each respondent also ranks the destination attributes, and the results are analysed. The relative importance of various destination features for different segments is determined in this way, and their managerial and marketing implications can be examined in the context of the subjects' media habits, because successful advertising depends on a detailed knowledge of a target market's reading and television viewing as a basis for deciding where to place the advertisements (Wind, 1978). Table 4.2 summarises the factors to consider in segmenting a market, and targeting communications or services to appropriate groups of customers by positioning the destination in potential visitors' perceptions.

An issue in segmentation research is whether to focus on actual behaviour, or clients' expressed preferences. Pragmatically observed behaviour can be assumed to be rational if it occurs consistently, but

Table 4.2 Segments, targets and positions for destination markets

---

Factors in market segmentation
* Measurable
* Accessible
* Substantial

Factors in identifying groups to target with marketing communications
* Destination preferences and choice behaviour
* Media habits
* Destination activities, length of stay
* Demographic, socio economic and psychographic characteristics
* Geographic location

Potential 'positions' for destinations to promote in communications

*	Stylish	___	Casual
*	Exclusive	___	Ordinary
*	Conventions	___	Backpackers
*	Exotic	___	Familiar
*	Accessible	___	Remote
*	Modern	___	Unchanged
*	Relaxing etc.	___	Energetic activities

---

the basis of rational choice for one consumer may be irrelevant to another person selecting between the same range of products. The overall holiday cost may be the critical factor for one person, while safety and comfort is a choice criterion which dominates other holidaymakers' choice of destination.

Many political or business leaders in many destinations have set objectives such as attracting higher-yielding business visitors, or longer-staying tourists in the belief that they create fewer negative impacts than traditional low-spending tourists. Conventions make up one segment regarded as suitable – they can bring together a thousand or more delegates staying in expensive hotels and patronising upmarket restaurants and shops. Consequently, destinations invest in the specialised facilities required for these activities, but pursuit of a specific market segment may conflict with other interests. The need for a convention and exhibition centre in Honolulu had long been recognised, but when it was finally approved by the State in 1993, the major hotels argued against the form of the proposal, because it incorporated an integral hotel as part of the centre, although their own occupancy rates were declining.

Destination imagery

Consumption decisions are influenced by marketing communications. The specific messages and images employed to stimulate consumption and to attract clients towards particular destinations at once reflect society's current values, and are a dynamic force in its development. The images used in marketing frequently emphasise the beauties of female and male human bodies, portraying them as vehicles of pleasure and self-expression in leisure settings associated with hedonism and display. While the use of these emotional appeals is not restricted to tourism many travel brochures offer explicitly sexual images which emphasises the importance of appearance. At the same time, a wide range of other consumer products are advertised by the appeal of physically attractive people displayed against the exotic attractions of distant beaches, mountains or great cities, thereby reinforcing the multiplex connections between health, tourism and general consumption decisions.

A content study of current advertising campaigns will show that destinations are promoted by emphasising a wide variety of primary or secondary features such as climate, scenery, welcoming people, colourful traditions, the range of activities, their exclusivity or other special attributes.

> Tourism is an industry based on imagery; its overriding concern is to construct, through multiple representations of paradise, an imagery (of the destination) that entices the outsider to place himself or herself into the symbol-defined space. . . .
>
> (Buck, 1993)

The effectiveness of image management techniques depends on an understanding of potential visitors' interests and attitudes towards the destination. Images can establish a meaningful position for the destination in the public's mind as being a place which is different from other destinations offering similar primary attractions. One beach resort may illustrate its brochures with pictures showing young children playing happily in calm, shallow water while their parents relax nearby. Another may depict a young woman being torn from a sailboard as a fifteen-foot wave curls over her. The images which these two resorts project make unequivocal statements about the type of visitor they aim to attract, and whose requirements they can best serve. Selecting which aspects of a specific destination to feature in the marketplace where tourists choose their holiday destination depends on two steps:

1 Identifying the resort's special advantages.
2 Understanding how to entice those visitors which the destination hopes to attract.

Fishbein and Ajzen (1975) have shown that the choice of a particular good or service is the result of a comparison of its perceived attributes with the person's set of preferences. Chapter 2 discussed ways of modelling tourists' choices at the individual level, but other forms of analysis are more appropriate for destination managers seeking to understand how to influence tourists' decision processes.

> From a practical standpoint, the more complete measurement of a destination image provides useful information for positioning and promotional strategies. For example if a destination is found to be difficult to categorize or is not easily differentiated from other similar destinations, then its likelihood of being considered and chosen in the travel decision process is reduced.
>
> (Mayo and Jarvis, 1981)

Using the responses to an open-ended question, Jamaica was categorised as a sun/sand destination by the imagery evoked of beaches, tropical climate, sun and ocean. However, the research subjects simultaneously differentiated Jamaica from other sun sand destinations by its negroid peoples and reggae music (Embacher and Buttle, 1989).

Many destinations suffer occasional adverse publicity resulting from political or natural events, and the resultant international media coverage reduces their attraction to tourists. Others have failed to achieve a planned level of tourism activity, perhaps because of low standards of service compared to alternative destinations. Appropriate image management can counteract the concerns which have kept visitors away, complementing practical programmes to restore the infrastructure, calm civil unrest or improve service standards. Since the goal of positioning strategy is to create positive and realistic images, image research can identify the issues which should be addressed in the subsequent marketing for the destination.

Fontayne (1991) has shown how a summary of current audience perceptions makes clear where marketing communications should be focused, to deal with misperceptions to be overcome or key selling points to be emphasised. As Table 4.3 shows, careful management of a destinations' marketing communications can result in an image shift which enhances the appeal of a destination or reduces negative impressions,

Table 4.3 Managing Singapore's tourism image

	Positive	*Neutral*	*Negative*
1989			
High awareness	Safe Clean Raffles hotel SIA	Chinese	Autocratic Censorship Modern Sterile
Moderate awareness	Restoration Good hotels Changai airport Good food	South East Asia Humid Tough on drugs	
Low awareness	New attractions Good shopping Public transport	Multicultural	
1990			
High awareness	Safe Clean Raffles hotel SIA Changi Terminal 2 Festivals	Chinese Very modern	Censorship Full hotels High rates
Moderate awareness	Good hotels Restoration Great food Hawkers Cruise port Multicultural New attractions Green belt city Tough on drugs	South East Asia Humid	Prime Minister Lee Sterile
Low awareness	Public transport		

Source: Fontayne, 1991 (modified).

increasing the likelihood that tourists will choose to visit it. However, any gains obtained by successful image management can be undermined by subsequent events. The adverse publicity surrounding the caning of an American visitor in May 1994 for spraying graffiti on cars in Singapore resulted in calls to avoid the destination, and to boycott its international airline, although traffic level was not significantly affected.

The effects of destination promotions

The images used to promote a destination are significant in other ways. Britain is often portrayed in overseas advertisements as a land of castles, cottages and hedgerows, where men wear kilts or bearskin hats, and people dance around maypoles. This is not consistent with most British citizens' perceptions of their country, and this type of discrepancy in representing a country can result in hostility or mistrust between residents, visitors and the businesses promoting a destination.

The way in which a destination is promoted also plays a role in structuring tourists' activities after arriving in a destination. Walmsley and Jenkin (1992), have observed that in New South Wales, towns have promoted themselves individually, 'but no authority seems to take responsibility for a regional perspective'. They recommended research into the distribution of tourist literature, and the way that visitors perceive distances and the relative locations of sites. An interesting contrast in the attractions offered to visitors to Britain and France during Channel crossings has been discussed by the National Economic Development Organisation.

> Ferry companies tend to present France in a very different way from the way in which Britain is presented. As an illustration, in the last year, Sealink Stena advertised the works of Monet and encouraged visitors to go to Giverney on the way to Paris, whilst P&O's French language short breaks brochure concentrated on British Cheeses, afternoon teas, 'le casque de bobby' and 'la milk bottle'.
>
> (NEDO, 1992b)

A variety of organisations promote particular destinations. These include hotels, airlines, and tour operators, many of whom may not be based in the destination, and each selects images which they believe enhance its appeal to their own clients. The way an organisation promotes a destination may conflict with the 'official' promotion line, or compliment it. One of the Hawaiian islands has been promoted under a variety of names, each valid in reflecting aspects of its varied appeal as the island of volcanoes and orchids for which it is renowned. However, these differing approaches at best diluted the effects of marketing for the island, and have resulted in confusion amongst the public about the distinction between the different islands in the State of Hawaii. It is now presented consistently by all advertisers as the Big Island, with its own logo. The text and imagery used in promoting it emphasise the range of attractions and activities it offers, and its greater size compared to other Hawaiian islands. However, many visitors still refer to it under one of its earlier identities, and at least one other island in the Pacific has recently begun to refer to itself in its tourism promotion literature as 'The Big Island'. A review of the lures used by states in America discussed the 'pithy and pleasing' slogans used in advertising. It found that 'State tourism advertising slogans fail to communicate USPs' (unique selling propositions), pointing out that within one State, there will be several regions which have little in common with each other. 'For instance, New York State has the Long Island beaches, New York City, the Catskills, and Niagara Falls. On the other hand, two or more states often share a single coherent region ...' Richardson and Cohen (1993).

The main responsibility for destination promotion lies with official bodies such as the NTO (national tourist office) (Akehurst et al, 1994). An NTO's responsibility is for its own area, and the tourist organisations within its boundaries. 'The whole tourist marketing message from an NTO's point of view is to identify primary, secondary and opportunity markets for the tourist destination's product, build up a communications system with these markets and to maintain and increase the destination's market share.' (Wahab *et al.*, 1976). Table 4.4 indicates the scope of promotional activities which NTOs undertake, both in the destination and in tourists' countries of origin.

NTOs are mainly funded by central government, under the philosophy that the benefits of successful destination promotion accrue to all its tourism businesses. 'The whole economy benefits ... and ... the taxation system represents the only practical way of collecting the necessary funds ...' (Jeffries, 1989). However, NTOs and similar public bodies often collaborate with hotels and carriers to raise additional finance, generally for specific programmes such as that discussed in case study J.

Table 4.4 Promotional functions of national tourist offices

In resort	In tourist origins
Welcome service	Joint marketing
TICs	Arrange familiarisation tours for travel staff and journalists
Promote individual attractions	Workshops for trade and public
Respond to individual visitors	Respond to consumer enquiries

Case study J

L'Angleterre Sud, une ile pour le week-end et autres escapades . . .

The SEETB (South East England Tourist Board) was concerned that the previously stable demand for holidays in Kent, Surrey and East and West Sussex might be disrupted by impending changes in the area. These included the opening of the Channel Tunnel, the completion of the Single European Market, and the greatly improved ferry services linking the continent and Britain on the short sea crossings. The threat posed by these changes was the loss of domestic short breaks, but the developments also presented new business opportunities.

A partnership was formed with Eurotunnel, all six Channel ferry companies operating at that time, 25 local authorities, 175 accommodation providers, 200 tourist attractions, two neighbouring Tourist Boards, East Anglia and Southern, and the BTA. The SEETB thus raised the finance and expertise needed for a new promotion. The objectives were:

- to produce repeat visits on short break visits by European motorists (the carriers' primary target);
- to increase the frequency of such visits;
- to produce new first time 'taster' visits by motorists;
- to achieve geographical and seasonal spreads throughout the regions, specifically dispersing tourists through the three tourist board regions, emphasising the shoulder months rather than the peak season.

Visitors who had previously been to London, independently or on a package, were the initial targets for the short break programme, because they were thought less likely to be deterred by driving on the left on Britain's roads. France, Belgium and The Netherlands were selected for the campaign, as German tourists were considered less likely to be interested in short breaks.

230,000 copies of an eighty-page brochure was produced in two languages, one in Flemish entitled 'Kortweg Engeland', the other in French, 'Angleterre Sud'. Each was written by professional

Case study J *(continued)*

travel journalists in the countries concerned. They promoted the South of England, its attractions and accommodation, providing informative descriptions of selected motoring routes through each county, and identifying points of interest keyed to clear maps, and illustrating each hotel in the scheme. Some of the brochures were distributed to campaign partners, and the bulk were distributed by three means:

1 Based on the BTA database of people who had contacted BTA offices in the previous two years asking for information on Britain, 66,000 were mailed direct.
    A pilot mailout was conducted in mid-1992, achieving a response rate of 60 per cent from The Netherlands, 55 per cent from Belgium and 46 per cent from France, thus showing that the database accurately targeted potential and experienced independent motorists to Britain.
2 A further 61,000 were handed to enquirers at BTA offices, or posted to them in response to requests.
3 A total of 33,000 were handed to enquirers at holiday exhibitions in Europe attended by many of the organisations participating, and at BTA promotions in each country.

The effectiveness of the promotion was investigated by research conducted after the 1993 season, to establish the performance of the programme, and as a basis for expanding the database for a subsequent campaign in 1994. The evaluation was based on 200,000 brochures, as this was considered a sufficiently reliable sample for tracking distribution. A short questionnaire had been bound into the brochures, and 8,000 of these were returned. A more detailed, four-page questionnaire was mailed to equal numbers of people who had returned the brochure questionnaire, and to those who had received the brochure but did not reply to the questionnaire it contained. 1,200 people were surveyed in each country (however, in Belgium 900 questionnaires were sent to Flemish speakers and 300 to French speaking citizens). 1,851 replies were received and analysed. The profile of respondents is shown in Table 4.5.

Case study J *(continued)*

Table 4.5 Profile of respondents to the L'Angleterre Sud survey

---

* 80% were between 25 and 64 years old
* Three quarters were married
* They were equally distributed by gender
* 90% had taken a short holiday in 1993
* Nearly three quarters had taken more than one
* 35% of the sample had visited the South of England
* The average length of stay was six nights
* Two-thirds booked their accommodation in advance
* Half of these booked through a travel agent, half direct
* 90% used the ferries
* Two-thirds travelled by car
* 65% visited the South East, 39% Southern and 20% East Anglian Tourist Board regions
* One in six used the discount voucher included in the brochure
* 97% wanted to receive the 1994 brochure
* 80% indicated they were quite likely to take a short holiday in England in 1994
* 39% said that although they had not visited in the current year, they might next year

---

It was estimated that those receiving the brochure had spent £35.5 million on accommodation on short breaks in the UK. Without the creation of the programme, between £700,000 and £1 million of accommodation spending would not have been generated, and ferry revenues from car crossings would have been £250,000 less. Table 4.6 shows how the value of the programme was calculated.

Table 4.6 Calculating the value of the L'Angleterre Sud promotion

---

Total brochure distribution	200,000
– of which, recipients visited the region	69,360
Average number of people in party	3
Total visitors	208,080
Average stay	6 nights
Average price paid per night	£28.50p

Total value of programme = 69,360 × 3 × 6 × £28.50 = **£35,581,680**

Case study J *(continued)*

Sources: based on Baker, 1994; Carver 1993 and disucussions with
SEETB managers.

Suggested exercise

Prepare a proposal for a collaborative campaign to promote your
region, and indicate how its effectiveness might be evaluated.

Package holidays and destination marketing

In contrast to an NTO whose role is to promote the region for which
it is responsible, 'a tour operator's allegiance to any destination is tenu-
ous' (Ashworth and Goodall, 1988). Inclusive tours represent solutions
to complex sets of problems for both clients and destinations. While the
familiar tour operators' brochures make it easy for clients to book all
the components of a holiday in a remote place, destinations obtain two
key advantages:

1 Tour operators bring a regular flow of visitors to destinations.
2 They overcome the difficulty destinations face of reaching out into
   the varied and diffuse markets from which their clients come. These
   features are set out in Table 4.7.

The significance of the package holiday concept in making travel
opportunities affordable and readily available to large numbers of
tourists should not be underestimated. However, tour operators are
highly specialised in moving clients from one origin to many destinations, and this puts destination-based businesses at a bargaining dis-
advantage because tour operators have obtained the initiative in
persuading their clients which destination to visit. In the face of competition between destinations, the variety of potential disruptions to
established tourist flows, and changing consumer tastes, NTOs devote
much of their overseas efforts to establishing relationships with tour
operators and retail travel agencies. This takes two main forms:

1 Strategic support is provided in the development of new areas or holiday concepts by providing introductions, influencing destination developments and legislative or financial policy.

2 Tactical effort goes into providing support to staff on familiarisation trips, through promotional events and the production and distribution of technical sales support literature or computer databases.

The relative market strength of tour operators, travel agencies and destinations in marketing holidays is a critical issue since 90 per cent of outbound British inclusive tours are sold by retail travel agents. Travel agencies dominate the supply of holidays within the traveller's origin area, and largely determine the information on which most clients make their selection of holiday destination. However, few travel agents are able (or willing) to stock the full range of brochures available, about 4,000 in Britain in 1993. What they decide to display to potential travellers reflects business criteria such as the different tour operators' commission levels, their reservations efficiency and the personal goodwill established with them over a period of time. The larger tour operators also select travel agencies to represent them in each market, deciding on the basis of their productivity.

A study of thirty travel retailers in the Reading area found a total of 15,015 brochures, representing 857 tour operators. All travel agencies

Table 4.7 Package holidays – features and advantages

To consumers

* Convenient purchase of all tourism elements
* Quality guarantees
* Protection through branding
* Convenient arrangements
* Reduced cost

To travel principals

* Tourists 'bundled' into economic groups for transport and accommodation
* Reduced marketing expenses
* Simplified booking and payment arrangements

To destination agencies

* Regular arrival of groups
* Predictable requirements
* Reduced marketing expenses

displayed a core of mass market brochures covering most popular destinations (Radburn and Goodall, 1991). Travel agency staff are trained in the techniques of selling from brochure pages and the computerised reservation systems of major tour operators, but this study found them ill-prepared to deal with travel enquiries outside the core packages. Although tour operators provide travel agents with marketing support, for example familiarisation visits to destinations for staff, few travel agencies undertake much marketing activity – 20 per cent took no action, and most just identified the range of holidays on offer by advertising in the local papers.

Against this background of *laissez-faire* destination selling, the importance of tour operators' brochures takes on a high degree of significance. They are one of the key factors in individual tourists' choice of destination, but destination managers have little influence on their content or style. The brochures of strong holiday brands (for example, Cosmos, Kuoni, Bales and Thomson) can readily be distinguished by their presentation, and their particular range of holidays, prices and styles. For a tour operator, the variety of destinations offered is a strength, giving its clients choice between the products it sells, but within any one brochure there is often near substitutability between the destinations it offers.

Brochures function by providing essential information about the destinations they feature in a consistent non-evaluative, easily assimilated way. Given their importance in tourists' decisions, it is interesting to investigate how accurately they represent a destination's attributes. Goodall and Bergsma (1990) found that skiing brochures gave short, focused overviews of each resort describing its attractions and features. The emphasis was on positive features such as the capacity of ski lifts, the drop of runs and their difficulty, but the study reported that inexact information was sometimes given, and it was insufficient to choose a destination appropriate for one's level of ability. This study also reviewed several tour operators' brochures featuring many resorts in common. 'No single characteristic is mentioned by all tour operators for all resorts. Generally, the more tour operators offer a resort the lower is the maximum proportion of operators including a given characteristic.' This finding can be understood as reflecting the tour operators' view of the importance of particular ski resort characteristics, but the study found no consensus as to what these might be. 'They exhibit varying but overlapping characteristics in different brochures.'

Half the brochures attempted some sort of grading for different types of skier. 'From the operator's point of view, this segments the market within a particular brochure. But some grading is inaccurate.' Of the ten using Les Arcs, for example, five rated it excellent for beginners, three well suited, and two considered it less suitable for them. A conclusion which can be drawn from this study is that how the tour operator presents the holiday components in the form of distinctive inclusive tours is more important in gaining sales than information about the resorts.

The overall result of tour operators' and travel retailers' marketing strength in the tourists' places of origin is that destinations become substitutable at the point of sale, because the emphasis is on the experiences offered by a holiday, or considerations such as its price, rather than the unique attributes of a specific place.

A destination communications-influence model

Destination managers have three particular problems to overcome in communicating with their clients:

1 Most are remote in spatial terms.
2 The culture within which their clients live is often relatively unknown to destination managers.
3 Focusing the promotional effort on those most likely to visit the destination is difficult.

The solution to these related problems is to rely on a variety of communications and distribution channels to reach clients in their origin

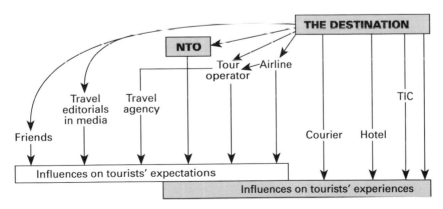

Figure 4.3 Destination communications channels and influences on tourists' expectations and experiences

countries. These are represented diagramatically in Figure 4.3. Consideration of the influences on customers' decisions reveals the restricted and indirect nature of the destination's role, the consequence is that its managers have limited ability to control both the way in which visitors learn about the destination, and what they are led to expect from their visit.

Rising expectations and destination quality control

The increasing familiarity of regular holiday-takers with a range of destinations has lead to pressure on destination managers to upgrade facilities and the general amenities of their resorts. This is expressed in comments (complaints, praise or casual remarks) while tourists are in their resort, or conveyed to destination managers through tour operators (and travel agencies) on the basis of clients' views expressed after their return, as indicated in Figure 4.4. Case study A has also indicated that destination managers seek the advice and assistance of established tour operators when deciding how to improve their resorts, and some tour operators have invested directly into resort development schemes in order to influence their scale and nature.

A common theme amongst marketers is to add value to their organisation's core offering. Just as an increasing range of family cars are now sold with anti-lock brakes and airconditioning as standard features, so are destinations investing in ways to enhance their visitors' experiences. Their approaches include general amenity improvements

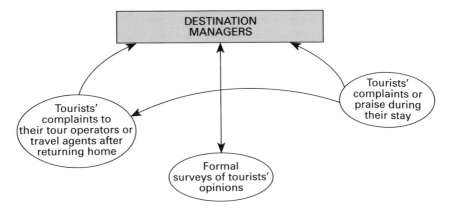

Figure 4.4 Feedback channels for destination managers

such as clean beaches and pedestrianisation schemes; improved visitor reception services including TICs, easier arrivals procedures, and multilingual staff; or setting standards for accommodation, catering, amusements and retailing enterprises and establishing training schemes for their staff.

Few NTOs actually own the products sold to tourists, and consequently their control over the standard marketing mix elements of price, product, promotion and place (distribution channels), is limited, compared to that of an industrial organisation. 'A large number of businesses generate a very wide range of tourist products, most of which are beyond the influence of an NTO with regard to volume, design, price, and promotion decisions' (Middleton, 1988).

One difficulty arising from this lack of control is that the standards promised or implied in advertisements may not be matched by the reality of visitors' experiences during their stay. This is significant because tourism is a service industry, in which clients cannot sample their destination before committing themselves to purchasing a holiday, and because the fragmented nature of the tourism industry means that many organisations are involved in delivering services to tourists during their destination stay, with the potential for lack of coherent service standards. Dissatisfied customers are unlikely to return, and furthermore, they share their unpleasant memories on returning home, and these negative accounts may dissuade their friends from visiting the destination.

The difficulties of co-ordination and control can also potentially undermine the planning of destination improvements or developments because these can be undertaken by a variety of developers with consultation and licensing restricted to physical aspects of the proposal. Destination development is discussed in the next chapter, but the point is significant for those promoting a destination because, as Levitt (1969) has shown, managers should focus on understanding what their clients want. 'People do not buy products, they buy the expectation of benefits. It is the benefits that are the products.' In most business situations, an organisation can determine its future product specifications on the basis of market research to discover what it is that its clients want from their purchases. Similarly, Kotler (1984) has called for a constant review of what businesses offer to their markets. 'The customer is looking for particular utilities. Existing products are only a current way of packaging those utilities. The company must be aware of all the ways in which the customer can gain the sought satisfaction. These define the competition.'

Figure 4.5 sets out a framework for destination marketing decisions. It highlights the need for market research to identify what tourists want from the destination, in the context of how they perceive its actual attributes and facilities, and of what they believe its potential to be (including undesirable developments). The destination managers' decisions about how to develop their area are taken in the context of their understanding of the desirable evolution of the area, given the present situation and the potential range of changes. Decisions also have to be taken about how to communicate the destination's actual features to potential tourists so that the people who are attracted to it will experience the forms of tourism which are offered.

Managers' attention is now being focused on the quality of tourist destinations, in the marketing, operations and planning of services. In many service industries such as banking, attention is now being focused on the quality of service which results for customers from planning, marketing and operations (Normann, 1991). Lockwood has explained it in the following way for hotels.

> Hotel companies are increasingly aware of the importance of quality and clearly use it in their advertising and promotion to customers and in the standards of performance set for their employees. There is still

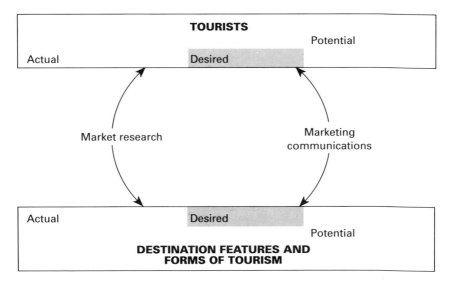

Figure 4.5 A framework for destination marketing decisions

however some confusion about what quality means. The hotelier should not be concerned with providing the best, but the best for his particular customers. The management of quality is not therefore just a technical problem, but a behavioural one too.

(Lockwood, 1989)

Tourist destinations systems have both *hard* aspects, in which a productive system can be defined to meet clear performance objectives, and *soft* elements, the human interactions in which problems are less structured, and therefore where the outcomes of actions are less predictable. These are termed 'messy' problems.

Problem situations, for managers, often consist of no more than a feeling of unease, a feeling that something should be looked at, both from the point of view of whether it is the thing to do and in terms of how to do it.

(Checkland and Scholes, 1990)

The effects of service failure become evident when clients complain to resort and hotel staff, or to tour operator and travel agency staff when they return home. Berry (1991) has examined the range of costs caused by quality problems. Three levels of management response to service failure can be identified (Lockyer and Oakland, 1981):

1 *Prevention* – training and planned procedures, to get the service right the first time.
2 *Appraisal* – routine inspection, and quality audits.
3 *Correction* – dealing with customers complaints.

It is critically important to ensure that the facilities and services promised in advertisements actually are provided to the tourists they attract. Unless their expectations are matched by their experiences, dissatisfaction will result, and to overcome these problems, destination managers have to convince two audiences of the significance of tourism:

1 Governments, to obtain infrastructure support and a policy framework;
2 Educating the public.

In a presentation to the Chartered Institute of Marketing Travel Industry Group in May 1994, The Honourable Wilberforce Kisiero, MP, Assistant Minister for Tourism and Wildlife, Kenya, explained that tourism now accounts for 40 per cent of Kenya's foreign exchange earnings.

It stimulates employment and local value added both in the formal and informal sectors of the economy. While a new tourism sector was being developed for low budget youth travel in Kenya, the main business objective was to encourage conference and cruise ship visitors rather than low yielding package holiday tourism. Similarly, new markets were being developed in the Far East and America to diversify sources of business away from Europe. In its current development plan, Kenya had embarked on an extensive training programme to expand participation and ownership in the industry, and to explain the importance of tourism and encourage wildlife conservation as a basis for tourism.

Destination promotion through special events

The regular promotion of a destination is sometimes replaced or intensified by a special-events approach. This may be based on an important centenary (the Armada) or the celebration of a famous resident or visitor (Dickens, or Captain Cook). Sometimes the interest in these events is strong enough to sustain a continuing campaign promoting that area. In other cases, the publicity benefits of a major event such as the Olympics decay, and have to be taken rapidly. Several reasons have been suggested for local or national government sponsorship of major sports events, trade fairs or international cultural festivals, as Table 4.8 indicates. Case study K examines the promotion of Nottingham, based on its connections with the mythical character of Robin Hood.

Table 4.8 The advantages of hosting special events

* Infrastructure improvements
* Amenity expansion and improvements
* Increased construction industry activity
* Enhanced civic pride
* Increase in real estate values
* Improved international (diplomatic) relations
* Increased international awareness of destination
* Experience of managing large numbers of visitors
* Potential for tourism development

Based on: Hall (1992), various tables.

Case study K

Nottingham and the Robin Hood promotion

Sherwood Forest and Nottingham Castle have a worldwide association with the legendary hero, Robin Hood. This provided a strong platform for a campaign to promote visits to the area, and to encourage a first visit to the area. By emphasising the Robin Hood connections the City and County Council hoped that people attracted by the legend would gain an appreciation of Nottingham's real features, and return later to enjoy the other tourist assets of the County. These include the many links with D. H. Lawrence and Lord Byron, and the area's association with the English Civil War and the lace-making industry.

A number of approaches were adopted to nurture the Robin Hood legend in 1991, the central factor which provided the focus and determined the timing was the potential for the City to benefit from the additional public awareness and interest resulting from two Robin Hood films released by Hollywood in that year. The publicity spin-offs included the theme tune 'Robin Hood the Prince of Thieves' which was number one in the UK charts for sixteen weeks.

Table 4.9 Nottingham's associations with the Robin Hood legend

* Nottingham Castle
* Sherwood Forest Visitor Centre and the Major Oak
* The Sheriff of Nottingham
* Tales of Robin Hood
* Robin Hood Festival in Sherwood Forest
* Robin Hood Pageant in Nottingham Castle

In order to capitalise on the opportunity, the area's associations with Robin Hood were identified (Table 4.9), they were developed for tourism, a media and consumer campaign was launched to increase awareness of them, and a complete package of accommodation and transport for visitors to book was developed under the banner, 'Live The Legend In Robin Hood Country'.

Case study K *(continued)*

The campaign was targeted at three segments of the tourist market:

1 Day visitors, defined as those living within two hours' driving distance of Nottingham.
2 Short-break family visitors.
3 Overseas visitors planning to visit Britain in the following year. Additionally, trade promotions were aimed at the coach and travel trade in the UK and overseas.

When they first became aware that the Robin Hood films were to be made, Nottingham's tourism officials contacted Hollywood film companies to offer historical advice and locations. Although the Castle is not medieval, and Nottingham Forest is quite small, the officers proposed that the film should be given its première in the presence of the Sheriff of Nottingham, a real post with a history spanning a thousand years, and since National Amusements Ltd had opened its first multiscreen cinema in Nottingham they supported the request and provided the commercial edge needed by the film's distributors.

In order to arouse interest, invitations were sent to the media accompanied by an arrow, and a signed scroll from the Sheriff. The day was carefully planned to present the most newsworthy aspects of Nottingham, beginning with a champagne breakfast for journalists at the 800-year-old pub, 'Trip to Jerusalem'. A local re-enactment group provided period atmosphere, raiding the pub to round up the journalists for a reception with the Sheriff. Then they were ransomed, and taken by coach to Sherwood Forest where interviews with the actors during lunch in a marquee were followed by a full combat jousting tournament. Later, 1,200 invited guests attended the première, and were greeted by a medieval guard of honour. The screening was followed by a private party in Nottingham Castle, with minstrels, fire eaters, and flaming torches.

Although Kevin Costner, the star of the film, was not able to attend (another of his films, *JFK*, was being made in Dallas at the time of the British première), Alan Rickman, who 'stole the film'

Case study K *(continued)*

according to critics in his role as the Sheriff, was flown in especially. The day achieved wide local and national publicity for the
idea of Nottingham as a new media centre, and highlighted the
potential of the Castle as a major function venue. The BBC world
service ran a half-hour programme, and the national press devoted
several hundred column inches to the Robin Hood programme.
Additional publicity was generated through photo opportunities
in the city, news stories and competitions. Journalists from
regional media were invited to sample Robin Hood weekends,
which were also offered to the papers as free prizes for reader
competitions. These were featured in nine newspapers, and
generated coverage worth £12,000 at advertising rates. (The story
was milked even further when later in the year Virgin Atlantic
flew the present day Sheriff to Hollywood to meet Kevin Costner
and to award him the 'key to Nottingham Castle' for his services
to tourism in the city!)

An advertisement entitled 'You've seen the film, now live the
legend' was produced for cinema audiences, and this was screened
free by Rank cinemas nationwide with the Robin Hood films.
The sixty-second commercial was also included as part of
Nottinghamshire's new promotional video.

Concurrently, new road links (including the M42 Birmingham to
Nottingham motorway) increased the population living within a
two-hour drive, adding 3 million potential day visitors. In order to
develop this market, 25,000 leaflets were printed, while an outdoor
poster campaign placed in the region linked the film and
Nottingham on pairs of adjacent panels. Local residents (and their
visitors) were stimulated by distribution of 427,000 A5 leaflets and
43 sixty-second radio spots on Trent FM broadcast through one
July week. Enquirers at Nottingham Tourist Information Centres
were given a free Robin Hood postcard when they bought a stamp.

In order to benefit from the interest created, a Robin Hood
product had been developed in collaboration with Nottingham
city and county tourism offices, managers of the main hotels, and
other private sector companies including Tales of Robin Hood
and Heritage Classics, a specialist ground-handler.

Case study K *(continued)*

The Robin Hood theme weekends offered a single Robin Hood rate of £25.00 per person bed and breakfast at the fourteen hotels participating in the 1991 promotion. A free information pack and discounted entry into the Tales of Robin Hood was included in the price. The County Council produced a brochure in collaboration with the hoteliers, with joint city and council funding of £16,200. The programme was nationally advertised and widely distributed, and generated £34,000 in extra hotel revenue, together with the additional spending in the city by its Robin Hood-weekend visitors estimated to be of at least equal value.

The programme was improved in the following year, when a banding structure was introduced to discriminate between the slightly differing facilities on offer by the hotels, the rates per couple were now set at either £39, £44, or £49. Six further hotels asked to participate in the programme. A joint project was established with British Midland on their scheduled air service to Amsterdam from the region to encourage combined transport and hotel bookings direct from Holland. Ten thousand leaflets were printed, and BTA staff were given familiarisation weekends.

Nottingham was awarded the British Tourist Authority's prestigious 'UK Tourism Marketing Award' (alongside Virgin Atlantic's Richard Branson) for its 1991 Robin Hood film campaign. In 1993, a similar, but lower-key première was organised for Mel Brook's spoof film *Robin Hood – Men in Tights*.

Sources: based on City of Nottingham documents and a presentation by Phil Nodding, Tourism City Tourism Manager, to the Tourism Society, 1993.

Suggested exercise

Devise a tourism promotion based on an event or character linked to your area.

Conclusion

The key to successful destination marketing is to identify a resort's comparative advantages across a range of holiday attributes to determine its market appeals. However, the fragmented nature of the tourism industry results in a lack of coherent promotional campaigns, where intermediate companies with strong customer contacts may choose to emphasise differing aspects of a destination's image.

Places become destinations only by attracting large numbers of visitors, that is to say that places become tourist destinations through being made into marketable products. Successful destination marketing entails projecting a clear image to chosen target markets, and offering clients satisfying product experiences which meet their expectations. Thus, marketing impacts on the client's decision process through promotional strategies, and has an important role in clarifying appropriate ways to develop a destination.

Further reading

Ashworth, G. and Goodall, B. (1991) *Marketing Tourism Places*, London: Routledge.

Crouch, S. (1985) *Marketing Research For Managers*, London: Pan.

Holloway, J. C. and Plant, R. V. (1992) *Marketing For Tourism*, London: Pitman.

Horivitz, J. and Panak, M. J. (1992) *Total Customer Satisfaction, Lessons From 50 European Companies With Top Quality Services*, London: Pitman.

Kotler, P., Haider, D. H. and Rein, I. (1993) *Marketing Places*, New York: Free Press.

Law, C. M. (1993) *Urban Tourism, Attracting Visitors To Large Cities*, London: Mansell.

Laws, E. (1991) *Tourism Marketing, Service and Quality Management Perspectives*, Cheltenham: Stanley Thornes.

Middleton, V. T. C. (1994) *Marketing In Travel And Tourism*, Oxford: Heinemann.

Suggested exercises

1 Contrast the descriptions of a specific resort contained in various tour operators' brochures with your own knowledge of it.
2 Justify to its residents the images and text you would use to promote your own area as a destination.
3 Draft a memo to a Japanese inbound tour operator explaining how to attract visitors from your local area.

4 Prepare an interview schedule to evaluate visitors' perceptions of a chosen destination, conduct a pilot study and modify the survey instrument in the light of your experience.
5 Discuss whether the 4Ps approach is adequate in understanding destination marketing.
6 Draw up a SWOT analysis of London for its tourism managers.

5
Policies for destination development

Introduction

The emphasis so far has been on existing forms of tourism and the contemporary effects of tourist activities on functioning destination systems. In this chapter, the frame of reference shifts, and attention is focused on the further development of destinations in the contexts of the forecast expansion of tourism worldwide, and the range of practical and ethical issues emerging as social (and political) concerns as the third millennium approaches.

'This book has argued that places become destinations through the development of facilities for their visitors': the implication is that a series of decisions must be taken about the type and scale of tourism facilities to develop, and about the appropriate role for tourism amongst other social and economic activities. This chapter investigates these decision processes, and examines the influences on the range of decision takers, considering for whose benefit a particular form of tourism development is intended.

The problems which tourism presents to managers, developers and politicians are those of interconnectedness, uncertainty, and ambiguity in the contexts of plurality, resource constraints and a persisting notion that tourism is a somewhat trivial activity. The systems model discussed in this book provides a framework to investigate both the range of inputs required for a particular destination's development, and the industry's effects on its various stakeholders. Investors, the construction industry, tourism employees and managers, residents and tourists are likely to experience different outcomes a result of particular developments. There can seldom be an equitable balance of outcomes between all these groups, but neither is it more likely that equity would result from the development of alternative industries.

The historical basis of destination development

Tourism, like most social activities can be more fully understood by identifying the events which led up to contemporary situations, and analysing changes in the relationships between key elements of the destination system over time. This approach is important for policy makers, whose task is to reconcile often conflicting interests in a consistent and forward oriented framework which recognises tourism as one component amongst many social and economic activities in an area. Table 5.1 lists ways in which the understanding of a tourist destination can be enhanced by setting tourism in its historical context for a particular locality.

Table 5.1 Insights gained from the study of a destination's history

* The factors which lead to the beginning of tourism to the destination
* The sequence of events in tourism development
* Why they occurred in that order
* The interest groups which benefited from tourist activity
* The early recognition of adverse consequences
* The particular interest groups which reported them

Based on: Pearce, 1980 (modified).

Rationales for the development of tourism

The development of a region's tourism sector can result from a variety of factors, irresistible pressures such as the government's need for foreign exchange, or pressure from airlines for the extension of an airport, itself resulting in the need for increased traffic to support their greater capacity, or residents' demands for jobs, often as a reaction to a decline in traditional local employment sectors such as agriculture or mining.

When faced with the decline of an area's existing industrial base, policy makers often turn to tourism because of the relative speed with which facilities can be developed, and the low cost of creating new employment in this sector. Previously depressed and derelict city centres such as Bradford's, or redundant docklands such as Bristol's have been revitalised by developing their potential to interest visitors. Defunct industrial buildings have been gutted and converted into museums or tourist attractions: the Canterbury Tales, a themed attraction presenting the story of pilgrimages to Canterbury is housed in a deconsecrated church. Worked out coal mines such as The Big Pit at Blaenarvon in South Wales have been made safe and are now presented as heritage sites demonstrating the old industrial skills and the working and living conditions of the area. Darnell *et al.* (1992) have described a related approach at Beamish, a living museum of traditional buildings, machinery and objects collected: 'to illustrate the historical development of industry and the way of life of the North of England'. Agritourism is another, often opportunistic response to crises in more conventional forms of land use. It has a wide appeal because Western society is concentrated in urban areas, and country excursions are a popular form of recreation. Such projects are, however, subject to the test of market place demand and compete with many alternative destinations. Table 5.2 presents a selection of additional reasons given in regional and national tourism plans for developing tourism.

Table 5.2 National and regional plans – reasons given for developing tourism

Economic
* Employment
* Foreign exchange
* Boost to other sectors

Social
* Cross cultural exchange
* Stimulation of new attitudes

Development
* Infrastructure
* Recreational facilities

Sense of national pride or identity
* Modernisation
* Traditional culture

Support for conservation
* Environmental
* Ecological
* Cultural

Auditing destination resources

Decisions about how to develop a destination are often based on research comparing present and potential market demand conditions, and an audit of the facilities which the destination currently provides. This exercise highlights specific development opportunities for a destination, and its tourism organisations. Typically it identifies a mix of investment requirements, in upgraded and new supply, staff training, and market promotion focused to stimulate demand for the new amenities.

Table 5.3 Matrix for destination development audit

| | Current | | | Potential for | | | | | |
| | | | | Improvement | | | Impact | | |
	Poor	Good	Excel-lent	Poor	Good	Excel-lent	Damag-ing	Good	Excel-lent
Primary features									
Secondary features									
Tourist infra-structure									
Business climate for tourism investors									
Staff skills and attitudes									
Marketing									

Table 5.3 sets out the basis for a destination audit. The approach enables the existing tourism resources of an area to be identified and quantified, while the potential for development of each can be assessed through market research to gauge demand, and by feasibility studies to evaluate the entrepreneurial opportunities. The final column allows each possible project in an area to be scrutinised for its impacts on the area. One of the concepts underlying systems theory is equifinality, an understanding that depending on the interactions of its elements and subsystems, a range of outcomes may result from a given system.

Similarly, each potential development project could generate various outcomes for the destination stakeholders. Despite the great number of tourist destinations, there are significant weaknesses in current destination research which make it difficult to predict the consequences of particular developments, as Wall and Wright (discussed in Butler, 1993), have indicated:

● the lack of a benchmark study from which to evaluate the effects of a programme;
● the difficulty common to all social sciences of setting up a control study.

There are also methodological difficulties in ensuring that any observed effects actually result from tourism rather than any other projects in the area, or more general economic and technological developments. These are important issues in a practical sense since tourism developments are themselves significant as components in the wider social, economic and environmental systems of the area. In turn, those local, regional or national plans act as powerful contexts to the decisions of tourism entrepreneurs and corporations. Similarly, the functioning, style and rate of development of tourism projects are themselves affected by the development (or lack of development) of commercial and industrial sites and the area's general infrastructure, including its roads, telecommunications, housing and so on.

There can be no full understanding of the interconnections which constitute the reality of a destination without taking a systematic view of the destination, yet the practical considerations of time and budget required for detailed research, and the commercial or political pressures on managers and planners limits the scale and scope of background studies.

Plurality and decision-taking in destination development

In most destinations, there is a wide spectrum of expert and public views about what needs to be done for the future, reflecting the variety of people with stakes in the area. An important reason for investigating the evolution of tourism is that the historical approach casts light on the way in which local interest groups tend to adopt polarised positions. Community action groups, ecologists, residents and others try to influence the form and extent of destination development proposed by investors. Typically, some advocate further development,

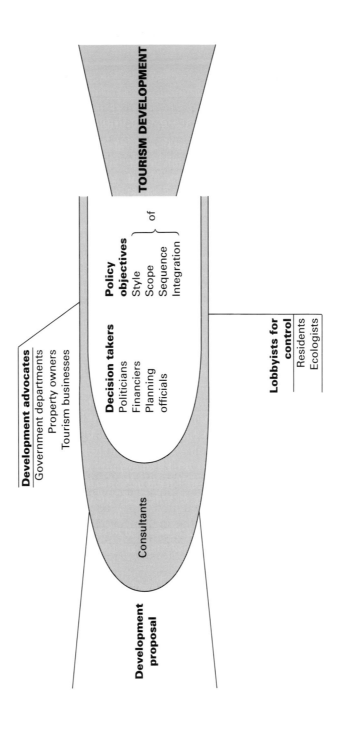

Development advocates
Government departments
Property owners
Tourism businesses

Decision takers
Politicians
Financiers
Planning
officials

**Policy
objectives**
Style
Scope   } of
Sequence
Integration

TOURISM DEVELOPMENT

**Lobbyists for
control**
Residents
Ecologists

Consultants

**Development
proposal**

Figure 5.1 Influences on destination development decisions

others opposing it, perhaps even arguing for a reduction of current levels of tourism activity.

The driving force in development is typically either an investor or the government, recognising profit or development opportunities, but Figure 5.1 shows the complex interplay of influences on decision-takers between development advocates and those who lobby for controls. Their views are often formalised and presented by consultants, and a dialogue develops between these experts and the advisers retained by developers and planning authorities. These exchanges take place in another context, the determination of policies both for the overall development of a destination, and for the scale and role of particular projects. The determining factor though, is the ownership of key elements in the destination. Figure 5.1 shows how these and other interest groups influence development policy and decisions. Case study L summarises the concerns of residents and the government regarding the (then) forthcoming resort development in a previously remote area of Hawaii popular as a retirement zone.

Case study L

Attitudes to resort development on the Big Island of Hawaii

In Hawaii, developers are required to submit environmental impact statements to the State Government as part of the planning process. Projections based on computerised modelling of the impacts of developments in the region forecast that 46,000 jobs would be created if all resort plans were fulfilled.

The resident population of the Big Island at that time was 111,800. Resort development would create a surplus of job vacancies above existing unemployment and this would create a demand for about 32,000 homes. In 1987 there were 43,000 housing units on the Island, with an average vacancy rate of 6 per cent. But in Kona, the main conurbation in West Hawaii, and the area where most developments were planned, only 1 per cent were vacant. The two employment growth sectors for the area are services and retailing. Both sectors are categorised in the West

Case study L *(continued)*

Hawaii Plan as 'dominated by lower wage jobs'. The cost of housing in the area is high, and with low wages in the tourism sector it is forecast that 75 per cent of all households might qualify for government housing assistance by the end of this century (*source*: West Hawaii Regional Plan). Table 5.4 summarises the resultant concerns expressed by the Government and by residents (see also Table 3.2).

Source: Laws (1991 modified).

Table 5.4 Concerns expressed over resort development proposals for the Big Island of Hawaii

1   Government concerns

*   Projected visitor forecasts suggest that demand will not support the expanded tourism stock at the prices intended by the developers
*   The region has insufficient residents to staff the proposed developments, and in general they lack the qualifications and experience for managerial jobs opportunities
*   All aspects of the infrastructure will have to be expanded to support the increased visitor and resident populations which will result from even partial implementation of the planned resort developments
*   The state and county will have to finance the infrastructure improvements ahead of any additional tax revenues which might flow from the developments

2   Residents' concerns

*   Increasing visitor numbers will result in congestion and related problems on the roads
*   The costs of house purchase or rental, and taxes (which are based on property market value) will rise beyond the reach of the present residents under the pressure of 'immigrant' workers' demands
*   Developments are sited around the most attractive beaches, and past experience of resort hotels suggests that access for local people will become more controlled than at present. The best beach areas tend to be 'reserved' for hotel guests, despite legislation intended to preserve the beaches as public areas

Sources: Laws, 1991 (modified). (Drawing on a public debate during State of Hawaii Planning Consultative meeting at Waimea, August 1988; and the correspondence columns of *West Hawaii Today* during August 1988).

Case study L *(continued)*

Suggested exercise

Taking the role of a resort developer, prepare three documents justifying your project to the investors, the government, and to local residents. Specify any assumptions you make.

Developers' perspectives on destination investment

Some development projects, generally those smaller in scale, are initiated by local entrepreneurs responding to the business opportunities which visitors' demands for services create. In other cases, an outside organisation which specialises in particular services such as catering, entertainment or accommodation may decide to expand by investing in facilities where it foresees development potential. These two factors, a developer's knowledge of an area and his commitment to it on the one hand, and his expertise in commissioning and operating tourism services on the other hand, can lead to four different outcomes, as Figure 5.2 indicates.

The investors who advocate tourism development may not be based locally; their lack of direct involvement in the community, and their involvement in other projects at the same time, raises the question of

Entrepreneurial skill	Entrepreneur's base	
	Local	**International**
Tourism specialist	Low budget Reflects local culture	Professional development Reflects international standards
General business	Low budget Modelled on foreign tourist facilities	Speculative development

Figure 5.2 Developers' tourism expertise and local sensitivity

their sensitivity to one project's effects on the community, and the area's economy, environment and ecology. This quartet of concerns lies at the heart of the approaches to impact evaluation which are increasingly regarded as central to all planning decision processes as the twentieth century draws to a close.

Local entrepreneurs with no previous experience of the tourism are likely to model their new business on others which they may have observed during their own travels. Often, their financial resources and access to business expansion funding are limited, and they will modify existing premises, adapting them more or less effectively as a shop, bar or restaurant for tourists. In contrast, a specialist firm is more likely to have professional design and construction experts, and to have a substantial equity base for its projects. These advantages are likely to result in the most modern facilities with higher standards of service, but their design and style may not effectively reflect the characteristics of the area. Opportunities for a specialist organisation to develop new tourist facilities in its own region are rare, but such a situation would be most likely to optimise benefits to the community and its visitors, striking a balance between high levels of professional competence and the sensitive use of the area's features. This situation also has the potential to create most employment locally since managers would not have to be brought into the area, and nor would profit leak away. Potentially the least satisfactory outcomes result from speculative investment in land or construction projects by companies which are based elsewhere, and which also have no operational experience of tourism services. However, the actual outcomes from a project also depends on the vision of the entrepreneur in creating a facility which is attractive to tourists, and which succeeds in providing satisfying services profitably.

A response to the varying quality and appropriateness of different developers is for the local authorities to set standards for development. One standard to which many destinations lay claim is restricting buildings to the height of palm tree, Table 5.5 presents a more formalised set of resort development standards.

It has been pointed out that demand flows in the tourism industry are highly volatile: visitors' are influenced in their destination preferences by events there such as war, natural disasters, or changes in exchange rates, while their propensity to travel is affected by employment levels, interest rates and many other domestic factors. The result is that flows of tourists between countries can vary abruptly. However,

Table 5.5 Standards for resort development

*   Density and height of buildings
*   Ratio of floor space to site areas
*   Coverage of site by structures
*   Setback from amenity features
*   Others
landscaping
open space
public access
parking spaces
signs
utility lines

Source: King and Whitelaw, 1992.

the decision to invest in destination facilities represents a long-term financial and managerial commitment to one place.

Clearly, it is not possible to uproot and relocate a hotel if the destination loses its popularity through changing local conditions, consequently its managers have the continuing task of attracting enough customers to sustain the business. In the case of a 500-room resort hotel where guests stay on average for two weeks, this implies generating bookings from up to 25,000 people a year, although as most tourism organisations anticipate less than full occupancy, a more realistic business target might be 20,000 customers. Typically, before such a project is undertaken, feasibility studies would be carried out for the benefit of the investor and the investor's financiers to forecast the probable levels of business which the resort will attract. A further element in financial planning is sensitivity analysis (Bodlender, 1991). The procedure is concerned with challenging the assumptions on which the financial forecasts were based, particularly the costs of borrowing capital, the effects of inflation on operating costs, and revenue from room tariffs and all other resort business activity. Revenue varies more or less proportionately to occupancy rates, and therefore sensitivity analysis can identify the effects of different numbers of clients on the resort's economic viability.

Most businesses located in a particular destination are dependent on the NTO (or similar agencies) for marketing to attract customers, and to create the demand conditions within which they operate, competing locally with similar enterprises. But even those large tourism companies which are represented in tourist origin countries will suffer a reduction in business if tourism to the destination is seriously disrupted by a strike or a storm. The small restaurants and shops which are a key feature of destinations are not able to overcome these adverse conditions, but hotels which are members of international groups may be able to switch clients already booked to properties located in other destinations. Although the original destination will lose revenue, the hotel group may be able to retain the financial benefits (and their loyalty as potential repeat customers) within the company.

Similarly, as was indicated in Chapter 4, tour operators present their clients with a wide selection of destinations from which to choose, but there have been many cases when holidaymakers who had booked a specific destination have been offered alternatives after local problems such as strikes, civil violence or storms. The consequence of switching group arrivals elsewhere is the loss of trade for all businesses located in the original destination. In contrast, other tourism plant such as aircraft or cruise liners (and their sets of crews) can be diverted if one particular destination loses its appeal, or when a route's profit potential is reduced through increased competition or changed regulations.

Government support for tourism investment

In many countries (or in selected regions of others) financial incentives are provided in order to attract inward investment, and to channel it to preferred schemes and locations. Grants or loans may be provided to seed projects which meet certain criteria such as those indicated in Table 5.6. Support can also take the form of an equity stake with profit share, or it may be in kind, for example, rent-free land. Even a straightforward loan can be important as evidence of the government's commitment to tourism growth. Other schemes offer low interest loans, guaranteed exchange rates and guarantees that profit can be repatriated. Sometimes it is possible to negotiate reduced tax rates

Table 5.6 Purposes of tourism investment incentives

---

* Accelerate development by increasing the speed of financial returns
* Remove obstacles to private sector profit objectives
* Positive discrimination in favour of preferred developments or regions
* Provide evidence of government commitment

Based on: Bodlender and Ward, 1989.

Table 5.7 Investment incentives for tourism projects in Ireland

European regional development fund	
Objectives	Assistance in attracting overseas visitors
Methods	Accelerate infrastructure provision
	Expand and diversify range of tourist products
	Increase scale of tourist developments
Eligibility criteria	Demonstrate ability to attract overseas visitors
	Show consistency with national tourism development priorities
	Provide public access
	Satisfy quality requirements
	Demonstrate harmony with local environment
	Demonstrate quality and extent of employment created
Assistance	10–50% of eligible expenditure
Agri-tourism grant scheme	
Objectives	Incentives to enhance rural areas for tourists
Eligibility	Individuals or groups of farmers (and others)
	Angling, theme farms, farm museums, heritage centres, pony trekking, etc.
	Provision of bedroom accommodation
	Restoration of old buildings
Marketing support	Equipment and material to support an approved marketing plan
Assistance	Grant aid up to 50% with a ceiling of £250,000, at least half on a farm.
International fund for Ireland	
Objectives	To improve the range of tourist facilities
	To improve lower grades of hotels and guest houses
	To assist community groups to develop amenities
Eligibility	Recreational and cultural facilities
	Provision of *en suite* bathrooms
	Small-scale all-weather leisure facilities in guest houses
	Enhancement of exterior appearance of the building to meet consumer perceptions of a typical Irish village hotel, or family guest house
Assistance	Grants up to 50% in respect of the Tourism Amenity Scheme
	75% for the community sponsored scheme
	33% for hotel and guest house scheme
Business expansion scheme	
Objectives	To help owners of tourism businesses to raise cheaper investment finance by securing outside investors' tax relief
Requirements	Investment by individuals paying Irish income tax purchasing new ordinary share capital without preferential rights in unquoted companies carrying on qualifying tourism activities
	The money raised must be used to create or maintain employment; enlarge trading capacity; acquire new technology; identify and exploit new markets; or increase sales.
Tax relief for capital expenditure	
Nature	Initial one off deduction for new premises or plant
	Writing down over a period of years for new and second-hand premises or equipment
	Accelerated capital allowance on new premises or plant.
Level of allowance	Normal rate: 10–20%
	Accelerated capital allowance up to 75%

Source: Bord Failte Investment Opportunities in the Irish Tourism and Leisure Industry, Dublin.

for an initial period. Table 5.7 summarises the range of support available in Ireland.

Various non-financial forms of support may also influence an investor to locate his project in one country rather than others. Relevant factors include priority access to materials which may be in short supply locally, for example building supplies during construction, or import licences for the goods which international tourists expect to find everywhere such as alcohol, or dairy products, even though they may be prohibited, or are not customary locally. Another deciding factor is guaranteed work permits for senior staff with critical skills, or the provision of training facilities for locally recruited employees. However, two other factors are crucial for investors in the tourism sector:

1 A generally supportive attitude towards tourism amongst policy makers, administrators and the community at large.
2 The economic and political stability of the destination country.

Development roles of national tourist organisations

Tourism cannot be treated as a self-contained activity, because of its interdependency with the other economic, social and environmental spheres which result from the varied activities it entails, as the British Tourist Authority has recognised. 'While tourism is essentially a private sector activity, the government recognises the importance of the present and future roles the industry can play in the economy as a whole ...' (BTA, 1985). Private sector development has generally been limited to projects offering good profit potential although they are often stimulated by government agencies, through investment incentives including grants or accelerated depreciation because of their employment creation or the likelihood that they will 'kick-start' other businesses. However, any individual project is more likely to succeed if the infrastructure is adequate, and this provides a strong rationale for public sector involvement in the development of tourism destinations (Holder, 1992). Because of the scale of development required, and its public good element, most infrastructure provision in destinations is determined and resourced by local or national government authorities.

National tourist organisations or administrations (NTOs or NTAs) have been defined as 'The authority in the central State administration in charge of tourism development at the National level' (WTO, 1979).

Table 5.8 Administrative roles of national tourist organisations

---

* Research, data collection and analysis
* Resource inventory and protective policy formulation
* Development of tourist facilities
* Manpower development
* Regulation of tourist and travel enterprises

Based on: Pearce, 1992.

In addition to their marketing functions which were discussed in the previous chapter, typical administrative roles for NTOs are listed in Table 5.8, and have been critically evaluated by Akehurst *et al.* (1994).

Planning decisions at the local level

Tourism plans at the national level are mainly indicative, due to the NTOs' limited ability to control their implementation, and this has had the result that 'few countries have been in a position to follow a policy of continuity regarding tourism development' (WTO, 1980). One reason for the NTOs limited control of tourism planning is the relative autonomy of local governments, although this varies from country to country. Overall, an NTO's status reflects the established political and administrative frameworks, boundaries and divisions of power in a particular country, and its goals are derived from broader government policies (Paddison, 1983). It is apparent from Figure 5.1 that development decisions are reached from a variety of political backgrounds, and Wanhill (1987) has found varying degrees of awareness of tourism amongst local representatives. Another level of complexity arises because the many managers involved in destination development have differing, even conflicting interests and approaches, as indicated in Table 5.9.

Public sector managers generally espouse long-term, socially responsive attitudes and values conditioned by their professional training, while their freedom to determine developments is limited because their role is to interpret the policy handed down to them by elected members of government, within legislative guidelines. Naturally, such limitations are not confined to the tourism sector.

Table 5.9 Philosophies of destination managers

Management function	Main focus	Time horizon	Professional values	Main responsibility
Development	Return on investment	Long term	Maximise investment	Investors
Conservation	Preservation	Current – defensive Long term	Scientific/cultural	Ethics
Planning	Equity	Long term	Legal norms/ technical standards	Social/political
Marketing	Tourists as customers	Current and future	Optimise tourist activity	Entrepreneurs
Facility management	Business activity and profitability	Short term	Efficiency and profitability	Proprietors

Adapted from: Ashworth and Voogd, 1990.

Research for tourist destination development projects

Every development results in impacts on the environment as buildings are erected, grounds landscaped and the area's resources are put to new uses, causing both physical and qualitative changes. However, when compared with alternative projects (including non-tourism use) each project has a specific set of relative advantages and disadvantages. Environmental impact assessment (EIA) is a method by which projects can be evaluated for their impacts in the context of local conditions. Goodenough (1992) has identified two aims of the (American) National Environmental Policy Act of 1970: decision makers should consider the environmental impacts of their actions, and the public should be informed of, and participate in the analysis of the environmental impact of proposed developments. Typically, an environmental impact assessment consists of a published statement which:

- identifies any inevitable adverse environmental consequences;
- considers alternatives to the proposed project;
- discusses the balance of short-term benefits to long-term effects on the environment.

Following 20 years of its use environmental issues and concerns are routinely considered as substantial goals in decision making. Furthermore, the environmental consequences of proposed actions are considered at an early stage in the development proposal.

(Goodenough, 1992)

Romeril (1989) has pointed out that the categories of effects which can be evaluated through EIA techniques should not be viewed in isolation, even though each may be the subject of specialist studies. 'Impacts in one category do not occur in isolation but interrelate ...'

At a more general level, destination research is concerned with understanding the general issues in tourism development. This often takes the form of studies analysing the nature of particular problems, or of policies towards them. Another approach compares the experience of two or more places, to discover differences and similarities, and then to account for the observations. The OECD commissioned a comparative analysis of twelve member states in order to investigate the circumstances under which tourism industry developments result in deteriorating environmental quality for host populations. The specific purpose of this study was to discover whether it is possible 'to design a tourist development policy that has no negative impact, and if so what would be the costs?' The findings suggested that local conditions are likely to deteriorate under four circumstances:

1   when a destination experiences rapid, uncontrolled growth;
2   where there are marked seasonal peaks in arrivals;
3   in areas with inadequate infrastructure;
4   where there is little planning and few controls (OECD, 1981).

An important weakness in the monitoring of developments was identified, the report commented that although some attempt was usually made to forecast the effects of a programme at the planning stage, there was seldom any retrospective review of what had actually occurred. 'Few developments, however have been subject to post-impact assessments or monitoring to determine if the impacts generated were what was forecast and planned for' (OECD, 1981). In the absence of that knowledge, planning remains an imprecise instrument in the goal of obtaining particular benefits from tourism, and avoiding its more harmful effects.

The differing purposes of destination research conducted by organisations in the commercial and government sectors can be supplemented by academic studies, both at a conceptual level and in examining specific examples, as Table 5.10 indicates. However, a disturbing feature of destination research is that many of the studies commissioned by tourism organisations are regarded as confidential and commercially (or politically) sensitive, and are not openly available, thus restricting our knowledge and understanding of complex, important phenomena.

Table 5.10 Differing purposes of destination researchers

	Research agent		
	Public	*Private*	*Academic*
Focus	Environment	Economic	Social
Timing	Pre-development		Post-development
Tone	Neutral	Positive	Critical
Breadth	Detailed	Focused	Less detailed
Context	Specific case		Case + general theme
Decision role	Major		Minor
Dissemination	Rare		Normal

Source: Butler, 1993.

Strategic planning for destination development

The discussion of marketing planning in Chapter 4 showed that the basis of the planning approach is prediction of the future, and its practice is concerned with co-ordinated responses in order to achieve predetermined goals. In its simplest form, a plan is little more than a set of action steps to be repeated, with due modification, in future planning cycles. However, Gunn, a leading advocate of the strategic approach to tourism planning has argued that: 'the concept of planning has shifted from making a *plan* (noun), to *planning* (verb)' (Gunn, 1988b). The significant difference is that strategic planning entails recognition of the complexity of change processes. 'Planning is concerned with anticipating and regulating change in a system to promote orderly development so as to increase the social, economic and environmental benefits. Planning is an ordered sequence of operations' (Hall, 1970, quoted in Murphy, 1985). The process of planning depends on estimating or predicting the future, 'Planning as a concept of viewing the future and dealing with anticipated consequences is the only way that tourism's advantages can be obtained' (Gunn, 1988). Fundamental to strategic planning, then, is a vision of what the future should be in order to define appropriate steps for action, and a strategy to enable a destination to achieve that vision, as case study M, of South Africa, shows.

Case study M

Tourism policies for South Africa

At the beginning of the 1990s, South Africa was contemplating the opportunities presented by the lifting of international trade and cultural sanctions after the abolition of apartheid by President De Klerk's government. The liberalisation of air regulation for both domestic and international flights also contributed to the generally greater acceptability of visiting South Africa as a tourist destination. Politicians regarded tourism as important in providing jobs, creating wealth, generating foreign exchange and contributing to regional development. However, the tourism industry suffered from fragmented, *ad hoc* marketing and development, and the international awareness of continuing violence in South

Case study M *(continued)*

Africa resulted in the cancellation of group bookings, and visitor arrivals remained disappointingly low.

In an attempt to exploit the potential of South Africa as an international destination more fully, the government published a White Paper on tourism in May 1992, setting out a strategic framework for the development of the tourism industry. This was based on consultation with those involved in tourism development through regional and national workshops held to identify the critical issues which needed to be addressed. The consultation process resulted in ten strategic guidelines which were presented for discussion at a second series of industry workshops around the country. The comments made then were the basis of the final document, setting out a framework for specific action plans at community, nodal, regional and industry specific levels. Domestic tourism marketing was to be carried out by regional bodies, while SATOUR (the South African Tourism Board) had the roles of international marketing, and facilitating private sector product developments. Five of the strategies are outlined below.

1 Regional inventories of tourism resources were conducted to establish a database disseminated through a countrywide network of TICs, enabling investment opportunities to be identified and prioritised. SATOUR provided advice to entrepreneurs, and financial support for accommodation schemes in important ecotourism areas.
2 The existing Hotels Act was repealed, resulting in the phasing out of mandatory registration. A voluntary grading and classification scheme developed by SATOUR in consultation with the trade was introduced. Hotel inspectors became 'standards consultants' under the new scheme, providing professional advice to members to assist them in improving facilities and service.
3 Guides.
4 A co-ordinated strategy on road signs to guide visitors more easily to tourist facilities was drawn up.

Case study **M** *(continued)*

5 A 'tourism culture' was promoted through newsletters, speeches and articles emphasising the importance of a responsible, balanced tourism programme.

In 1994, the first free, democratic elections were held in South Africa. Contemplating the tasks which would face them after election, the ANC foresaw important social, economic and diplomatic roles for tourism. Their advisers forecast that, if managed successfully, international tourism could generate £1.3 billion in foreign exchange, support up to 1.4 million South Africans and build understanding amongst different people.

The ANC was critical of the South African Tourism Board's previous strategy of allocating a significant proportion of its funds to trade support rather than consumer promotion. They believed that this had contributed to the poor performance of the industry, noting that Australia received five times as many visitors, although it is remoter from European and American markets, and more expensive than South Africa. The ANC recognised that South Africa's problems stemmed from its long and debilitating period of international isolation, resulting in declining service standards since many of the country's hotels had been forced down market in the attempt to capture domestic business to replace weak international demand.

The ANC regarded the keys to tourism success as aggressive consumer promotion and marketing based on a sound vision, a research programme and a dedicated tourism database which would form the basis of a ten-year plan to develop the industry. They recognised that the most successful tourist destination in the world is man made – Disney World in Florida. It receives more visitors annually than any other destination, and the ANC planned to create a pavilion within Disney World, so that South Africa could take its place amongst other countries represented there.

A few weeks before the 1994 elections, Peter Mokaba, Chairman of the African National Congress Tourism Forum, discussed the importance of tourism in the new South Africa. The

Case study M *(continued)*

following notes draw on the views he put forward at a seminar (see also the Preface to this book).

If the new government were to set itself a target of 1 million additional tourists annually by the year 2000, South Africa would need to expand its tourism infrastructure by 18,000 rooms in new hotels and game lodges, and purchase 200 new luxury tour buses. Airport and peripheral services will also need to be expanded. The stakes are high, but the impact on the local economy would be staggering, creating an additional 150,000 jobs, thereby supporting a total of about 1.4 million people. Approximately 7 billion rand would be earned and the construction industry, which is the key to our housing construction plans, would be kick-started.

Tourists are seeking more interaction with the natural environment, surveys indicate that 90 per cent of visitors are attracted by South Africa's natural, scenic and wild life elements. This a major lever in the quest for further development of international and domestic tourism. But the natural attractions only remain a draw as long as they can be preserved and managed successfully, and future funding for environmental management is a cause for concern. Tourism could act as a major catalyst for environment conservation through private and semi-private tourism interests. In addition, we need to determine the tourist carrying capacity of wild life parks, and develop new tourist attractions. Within the conservation ethic, hunting will have its place, and will be administered and managed as part of the ecoresource.

Some of the most bitter opponents of conservation have been the people who live in and around ecotourist destinations. They have been forced off their land on to inferior land to make space for affluent tourists, and the wildlife they want to look at. Without consulting the communities, and including their interests meaningfully, ecotourism will never develop its full potential.

The communities must be made to realise that the development of the ecoresource can feed more mouths, create more jobs

Case study M *(continued)*

and earn more foreign currency at a better unit invested to unit return basis, while simultaneously contributing to the establishment of political and economic order and security in the townships and the country. Endemic crime and violence in South Africa has not been conducive to inspiring tourism confidence, but tourism can help to enhance appreciation among communities of the moral importance and value of peace, tolerance and good will. It is the only industry which can make inroads on the rural unemployment problem in the country, within a reasonable time frame. Tourism thus constitutes an incentive to bring about peace and security, and is a powerful economic instrument with which to defend that peace and security.

The tourism industry requires interaction between several government departments, trade and industry, foreign affairs, environmental affairs, transport, water affairs, forestry, national and provincial park boards, and the local authorities. As such, it needs a single dedicated ministry, its powers undiluted by the burden of multiple portfolios. The new tourism ministry will be concerned with international tourism strategies, the creation of the Tourism Capital Development Bank, the development of regional and nodal structures, and interaction with civic organisations, trade unions, taxi associations and other groups involved in tourism.

Communities must benefit from tourism in a direct and active sense. The creation of a network of home-based bed and breakfast facilities will benefit households in both urban and rural areas, these can be regulated and controlled by local government, with relevant levies imposed and collected. A maximum number of tourist beds per household would be set by the provincial tourist board, and the rooms themselves would remain private, but registered with the local tourist office, which would print and distribute brochure listing accommodation available to tourists. Tourism is a bridge builder of understanding amongst people and an effective mechanism of cultural exchange, the communities will thus not only benefit materially, but also spiritually through active and increased tourism.

Case study M *(continued)*

It is not going to be easy to market South Africa in a tourism sense, given the many years of isolation and boycotts, and the habits they have developed. But by restructuring and revitalising our tourism industry, broadening its participative base, creating new and varied products to overcome the image we have at present of being a 'one product destination', marshalling our existing anti apartheid forces abroad to play a new role of assisting in promoting this country, and embarking on dynamic marketing both within and without the country, the potential exists to transform South Africa into a tourist destination without equal. The formation of a regional tourism authority for the countries of Southern Africa is critical to effective international marketing.

The funding for restructuring and development could be sourced in a number of ways. The new government will have to take the lead in leveraging public monies, with contributions from the industry itself, initiating joint synergistic marketing efforts with the private sector and offering incentives to development, either through cash grants, tax allowances or judicious use of the issuance of gambling licences which will be awarded with great circumspection, as a national asset through a system of open tenders, and will be linked to the promotion of international and domestic tourism.

Tourism, as a matter of policy, should aim to increase employment and entrepreneurial opportunities among all our people, it should make provision for the training and education of those people and their communities to develop their full potential; it should be a major foreign currency earner and foreign trade booster; it should generate development in the less developed areas of our country; it should unleash the stifled energies and potential that can be generated by healthy competition, by combating monopolies without demoralising the large but non-monopoly corporations involved in the industry; it should develop and expand the necessary infrastructure to support tourism projects.

Case study **M** *(continued)*

On the day before Nelson Mandela was inaugurated as South Africa's President, the South African Ambassador to the Court of St James, His Excellency Kent Durr, addressed the Chartered Institute Of Marketing Travel Industry Group at a meeting in London. Mr Kent Durr had previously held the post of Minister of Tourism, and he said:

> A new democratic South Africa has the opportunity to pro-mote further plans to unlock South Africa's tourism potential. ... There is no question that the new government will respond dynamically to the many opportunities opened up. Particularly since the leisure and hospitality industry is one of the most rapid and cost effective engines for job creation. ... The provin cial dynamic, with nine new provinces will probably also be heightened with each region also seeking to capture its share [of tourism]. ... In the nature of things there will be a need for national co-ordination and leadership as well as struc-tures for sub continental and international packaging and promotion. ...

Sources: presentations by officials of the ANC, SATOUR, Ambassador Kent Durr, and SATOUR documents.

Suggested exercise

Brief the newly elected Prime Minister of a Third World country preparing a speech in which he (or she) will explain to the population why a significant proportion of the national econ-omic resources are being devoted to projects for tourists from overseas.

Emerging tourism policy paradigms

Inskeep (1993) has conducted a detailed study of national and regional tourism planning for the WTO, finding that they shared concerns for coherent policy, a balance of environmental, socio-cultural and economic objectives, and sought realism in the face of market demands. Table 5.11 summarises his conclusions.

National tourism development plans must also span a period of time during which policy can be put into effect, and they must encompass the spatial aspects of its implementation around the country. Lim (1993) has explained how the Philippine Tourism master plan has been structured in three main parts, to deal with these requirements.

1 *Long range master plan* – aims to distribute the benefits of tourism throughout the archipelago, by developing tourism clusters, each with an international gateway.
2 *Medium term development programme*.
3 *Destination area plans*.

Planning may create problems in those areas where tourism development is anticipated, bringing the opportunity for speculative land acquisition, or imposing a rigid structure which inhibits the innovative and flexible development that characterises many successful destinations. Other difficulties result from planning which has been conducted in a narrow frame of reference, without taking a systemic view of the economy, ecology and social realities of the area. Many current tourism plans emphasise forms of tourism which are regarded as acceptable solutions to the range of problems which destinations can experience, and seek to control the growth of tourism for the reasons indicated in Table 5.12.

The recurrent use of the terms, 'green tourism', 'sustainable tourism' and 'ecotourism' indicates a growing awareness of the negative impacts of tourism by politicians, journalists, tourism managers, planners and academics, and a growing belief in controlling the type and scale of tourist activity in destinations. However, such policies are not simple to implement because they depend on tour operators attracting clients who are willing to accept the forms of tourism desired by destination managers.

Hawkins (1993) has pointed out that the corollary of promoting tourism as the world's largest industry, is the task of convincing national governments to adopt policies reflecting its importance, and concluded

Table 5.11 Good practice in national and regional tourism planning

* Carefully planned and managed destinations are more likely to be successful than unplanned areas
* Planning provides guidelines to less developed countries for commencing tourism on the right track
* Planning redirects tourism in established areas to be more beneficial
* Effective planning must be based on sound methodological approaches, with the application of a sequential planning process
* Quality tourism development implies protecting the environment, maintaining cultural identity and achieving high levels of tourist satisfaction while still generating economic benefits
* Destinations should select the combination of tourism forms which are most appropriate to the area
* Planning principles include establishing tourist gateways, staging areas and zones, clustering attractions and staging development
* Marketing and product development must be carefully co-ordinated
* Community involvement in tourism is now recognised as essential
* Tourism is being integrated into national and local economies
* Effective planning requires not only procedures and techniques, but also political commitment and strong leadership
* Pilot projects can demonstrate how new forms of tourism and development approaches can work
* Public – private sector co-ordination is an essential ingredient in implementing plans successfully
* Investment incentives (and disincentives) can be useful in implementing investment strategies
* Education and training is essential for successful tourism, both for staff and the general public
* Tourists must be informed about their destination, and encouraged to respect it
* National and local government must often take the initiative in setting quality standards for tourism development
* Continuous monitoring is essential

Based on: Iniskeep, 1993.

Table 5.12 Reasons for controlling the growth of tourism

* Allow residents to adjust
* Balance with infrastructure development
* Integrating with the development of other economic sectors

by saying that dissatisfaction with the existing administration of tourism is leading to new paradigms, a different way of thinking about tourism resulting in the search 'for more direct responses to local wishes, a negative reaction to economic development and wealth distribution policies, and a switch to long term planning of social and environmental concerns'.

The justifications for a planning approach are that tourism is a new activity, that co-ordination is necessary to ensure that all elements are developed in an integrated manner to serve community and tourist needs without compromising environmental, and socio-cultural needs. Planning can optimise the benefits and reduce the problems resulting from tourism activity, and ensure that the natural and cultural resources for tourism are not destroyed or degraded in the process of development. But it is pointless to plan for tourism without at the same time taking into account the detailed needs of all stakeholders in the area, and the ways in which tour operators attract their clients to the destination, and manage their experiences of the area.

By reconciling environmentally responsible demand-side action with supply-side policies which explicitly acknowledge resource values and constraints, the strategic approach emphasises synergistic solutions. By capitalising on resource-based opportunities to develop partnerships between the various interest groups, host communities, governments

Table 5.13 Guidelines to aspiring destinations

1   Make residents aware of the advantages of tourism, demonstrating economic benefits and encouraging them to share tourists resources and amenities
2   Base tourism planning on goals identified by local residents so that they can maintain their lifestyle, keep developments within local carrying capacity, and match the pace of change with local desires
3   The images used in the promotion of local attractions should be endorsed by residents
4   Co-ordinate public and private efforts to maintain local opportunities for recreation
5   Retain respect for traditions and lifestyles through local involvement in tourism development
6   Local capital, enterprise and labour should be invested in local tourism developments
7   Broad based community participation in tourism events should be encouraged, as it is local residents' homes which are being put on display
8   Destinations should adopt themes which reflect history and local lifestyles and enhance local pride in the community
9   Mitigate local growth problems before increasing tourism activity as tourism is an agent of change

Source: D'Amore, 1983.

and industry, strategic destination planning emphasises the advantages of attracting market segments which match the range of attractions and amenities the destination can provide. D'Amore has proposed a set of 'guidelines to aspiring destinations' (Table 5.13) which draw together many of the points established in this book.

The goal of every organisation involved in the tourism industry must be to develop new forms of tourism which will bring the greatest possible benefit to visitors, the host population and tourism business, while minimising any harmful consequences to the destination's ecology and culture, as Pigram (1990) has pointed out. He argues that: 'environmental degradation is rarely catastrophic, but typified more by cumulative threshold effects'. Since tourism is a fragmented, complex and evolving industry, such programmes can only succeed under one of two administrative regimes in destinations, directive centralised control, or democratic co-ordination and public–business partnership. In turn, these frameworks for strategic planning depend on a detailed understanding of the nature of tourist activities and their local effects, and of the differing consequences of the varying forms in which tourism is organised for destination systems.

Conclusion

This book has been concerned with the effects on destination areas of the predominant modern form of tourism, the mass market for packaged holidays characterised by charter flights, branded tour operators' brochures and a marketing pitch based on consumer price sensitivity. Evidence has been presented that the familiar form of mass tourism has sometimes damaged the environment, ecology or culture of destinations, and it has been suggested that the economic gains of tourist activity are sometimes creamed off to the detriment of local amenities and residents.

Recently, new forms of tourism management and new priorities in destination development have recognised these concerns, and responded by adopting a long-term view of the future, both for tourism and the destination. A more open and comprehensive consideration of the destination as a system enables planners and decision takers to recognise the differing interests and concerns of everyone with a stake in an area. The concern of modern destination managers is to formulate more encompassing and ethically-based policies for local development and to express preferences for more sympathetic forms of tourist activity and tourism organisation. Chapter 6 examines these and other issues in detail as they apply in the case of Dubai.

In summary, it seems that a consensus is emerging in favour of planning or partnership approaches to destination development. This takes the form of a dialogue between government agencies at all levels, the various organisations involved in creating and delivering tourism services, tourism industry employees, destination community residents, and groups representing special interests such as ecology and the environment. Research into destination management issues and policies is improving our understanding of many specific social, economic and environmental or ecological effects, while examination of the destination as an open, soft system helps to clarify the interrelationships of functioning destination subsystems.

But holidays are expensive discretionary purchases. Unless the forms of tourism which destinations and tour operators offer to the public are enticing, and their experiences of destination places, people and activities satisfy visitors, a destination has little prospect of sustaining its tourism industry in the future. Therefore, the final word in shaping the future of the tourism industry lies with tourists, who express their views through selecting destinations (and tour operators) which provide the type of experiences they seek, and by not returning to those which they have disliked.

If the consensus amongst destination communities, travel companies and governments is to respect, preserve and enhance the unique qualities of each, its environments and cultures, then the crucial task is to educate tourists to avoid those areas where tourism is organised in an exploitative and damaging form, and to encourage them to visit those destinations which have adopted positive policies and forms of tourism which emphasise the beneficial aspects of tourist activity.

Further reading

Gunn, C. (1988) *Tourism Planning*, 2nd edn, New York: Taylor & Francis.

Iniskeep, E. (1993) *National And Regional Tourism Planning, Methodologies and Case Studies*, Madrid: WTO.

Lickorish, L. J. (1991) *Developing Tourism Destinations, Policies and Perspectives*, Harlow: Longman.

Pearce, D. (1992) *Tourist Organisations*, Harlow: Longman.

Poon, A. (1993) *Tourism, Technology and Competitive Strategies*, Wallingford: C.A.B. International Press.

Richter, L. K. (1989) *The Politics Of Tourism In Asia*, University of Hawaii Press.

Theobald, W. (ed.) (1994) *Global Tourism, The Next Decade*, Oxford: Butterworth Heinemann.

Suggested exercises

1 Evaluate the strengths and limitations of the general destination systems model introduced in Chapter 1.
2 Draw up an outline Environmental Impact Statement for a major tourism project in your area.
3 Interview a politician and a destination manager to gain contrasting perspectives on the role of planning.
4 How should one decide on an appropriate role for tourism in a given locality? Who should take this decision?
5 Draft a letter from a major resort developer to the Prime Minister of a small island state, setting out the final terms on which he would agree to site his project there.
6 Draft the Prime Minister's response.

6
Tourism in Dubai

Introduction

Dubai is one of the seven states which comprise the United Arab Emirates. It consists of a modern city lying on the southern shore of the Gulf, backed by desert. Its visitors can enjoy modern amenities and sample traditional Arabian experiences. This chapter draws on various reports and interviews with senior officials and managers to describe the significance and development of tourism in the context of Dubai's particular social, economic and religious conditions. Figure 6.1 illustrates the extent of the City's growth.

Dubai's tourism facilities and attractions

The major features of a visit to Dubai can be established by conducting a content analysis of its trade manuals or promotional literature. These emphasise the opportunity to experience aspects of an Arabic way of life, Dubai's tolerant and safe environment, good international hotels with varied night life and swimming pools which are heated in winter and chilled in summer, shopping in modern malls and the souks, championship grass golf courses, desert safaris and dinner amongst the dunes, and unpolluted beaches with calm, warm seas. Dubai itself has few ancient sights, but travel agents recommend that tourists use its hotels as a base to visit the other Emirates. During the European winter, the climate is 'near perfect', and Dubai is easily accessible to

a) Dubai, mid-1950s

b) Dubai, 1994

Photo courtesy of DCTB.

Figure 6.1 The development of Dubai

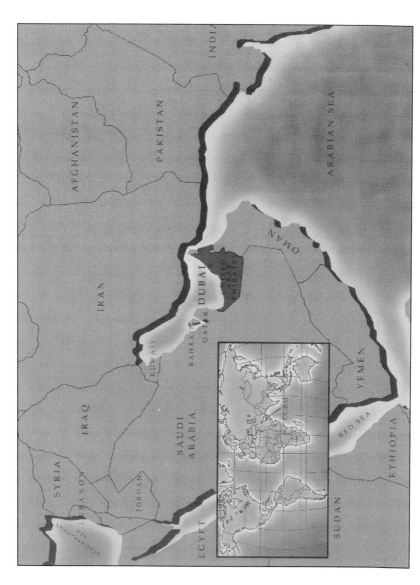

Figure 6.2 Dubai's location

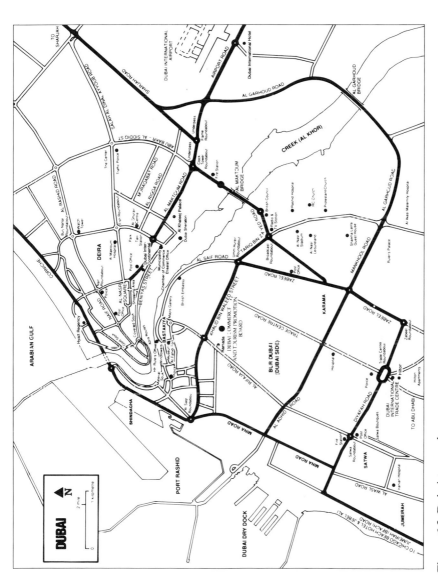

Figure 6.3 Dubai town plan

travellers, lying midway between Europe and the Far East, with good air connections (see Figure 6.2).

A brief history of Dubai

Originally a small fishing and pearling settlement, Dubai was taken over in 1830 by the Maktoum branch of the Bani Yas tribe, who still rule. Their liberal attitudes made it attractive to traders from Iran and India, and it developed as a centre for regional commerce. It became a British protectorate as part of the Trucial States, and in 1972 these states gained independence and formed the United Arab Emirates, each Emirate retaining a high degree of autonomy over its internal affairs. The discovery of oil in 1966 has dramatically transformed the state, as the ruler at that time, His Highness Sheikh Rashid bin Saeed Al Maktoum, had the vision to invest the resultant wealth in the rapid and comprehensive development of Dubai's economic and social infrastructure, laying the foundation for a modern society. Kay (1987) states that 'all the roads, all but one hospital, and nearly all the schools have been built since' the discovery of oil.

Dubai is now a modern and rapidly growing city, surrounded by sand desert rising to high and arid mountains, the traditional home of nomadic Bedouin who have all been resettled in modern villages in small oases, where many choose to continue farming camels, sheep and goats and dates. The population has increased rapidly as a result of improvements in housing, medical care and the growth of a diversified economy. In 1900, the population was estimated to be 80,000; the first census in 1968 recorded 180,000. By 1992 the population had risen to 529,000, about two-thirds of whom were expatriots attracted from the Indian sub-continent, the Philippines, Iran, other Arab states, Europe and America, by Dubai's safe and prosperous environment. World Bank figures confirm its prosperity, the per capita GNP for the UAE was US$20, 140 in 1991, compared, for example, with US$7,820 for Saudi Arabia. The business supplement to the *Khaleej Times* (3 November 1993) reported that Dubai came unscathed from the Gulf War and other regional crises, enhancing its reputation as the safe gateway to the Middle East for entrepreneurs, industrialists and investors.

Dubai has been Islamic since the lifetime of the Prophet Mohammed, and the continuing importance of religion in the daily lives of nationals (Arabs) is evident in the many new mosques, the daily observance of calls to prayer, and Ramadan. In contrast to most other countries in the region, a significant feature of Dubai for the continuing development of tourism and international trade is its tolerance of foreigners' religious and social beliefs and customs. One of the slogans used in Dubai's promotional literature is 'where East meets West', referring both to Dubai's location and to the cosmopolitan life style of a state where two-thirds of the population are expatriots.

The development of Dubai's industry and commerce

There are 52 per cent of Dubai nationals under 15 years of age, and one of the Government's priorities is to create suitable employment opportunities, it recognises that oil is a finite resource, and developments for the future are based on Dubai's pro-business attitude. The state has a major man-made deep water port, a modern air cargo terminal and a Free Trade Zone. Together, these serve the Middle East with legal and banking services, and regional re-exports. Foreign companies are welcomed, but need a local (Arab) agent or patron, unless they are established in the Free Trade Zone where incentives encourage multinationals to establish business operations. The Free Trade Zone was established in 1985. Table 6.1 shows the origins and operations of the 503 companies already established there by July 1993.

One of the keys to Dubai's economic success is the search for all possible synergies, recognising and harnessing the linkages between its various sectors. The Jebel Ali Free Trade Zone creates employment, supplies goods to local enterprises and (in 1992) purchased £270 million of goods and services from local suppliers (*Jebel Ali Review*, 1993). Another example of how Dubai gains the maximum benefit from projects is the modern aluminium smelter. This plant is sited adjacent to a natural gas complex which supplies its power, and free gas to generate Dubai's electricity. The excess heat from these activities is used to desalinate 22 million litres of water daily. The rapid increase in population, industrial requirements, the construction industry and the growing agricultural sector all increase the demand for water, which is further exacerbate by a policy of building recreational parks and other improvements to the city's amenities.

The need for a dedicated air cargo terminal had been identified during the 1970s and 1980s, a period of intensive construction in the Gulf triggered by the wealth created from oil exploitation. Airlines returning to Europe and the Far East's industrial centres had empty cargo

Table 6.1 International companies established in the Jebel Ali
Free Trade Zone

No.	Origin	No.	Type of business
186	Middle East	161	Manufacturing
128	Indian sub	143	Wholesaling
107	Europe	117	Trade
44	Far East	82	Services
28	N. America		
10	Other countries		

Source: Jebel Ali Review, July 1993.

space, and manufacturers from South East Asia began to freight cargoes
by sea to the region, then use cheap air cargo space to service their
markets in the Middle East and Europe, gaining both speed and economy in their distribution systems.

The Dubai Cargo Village was opened in July 1991, construction
having continued throughout the Gulf War. The Cargo Village is 15
minutes by road from Dubai's 74 berth sea port, and 45 minutes from
the Jebel Ali Free Trade Zone, and is linked to them with a fleet of
bonded vehicles, offering traders a 'No fuss no red tape' connection.
The Cargo Village can service four 747 freighters simultaneously, and
currently has a 250,000-tonnes annual capacity, with the potential for
expansion to 450,000 tonnes. In its first year of operation it handled
169,930 tonnes, and it won the Best Cargo Airport award at the
International Air Cargo Forum in Luxembourg in recognition of its
integrated facilities (*Cargo Village News*, September 1992).

Tourism in Dubai

A tourism manager interviewed in Dubai pointed out that the oil boom
has endowed the country with excess hotel beds and airline seats, and
therefore it had been logical to develop a tourism industry. Tourism
accounts for 1 per cent of Dubai's GDP, but its importance is expected
to increase because of the synergy with other aspects of Dubai's economy, and because it is valued as a clean industry offering a wide range
of employment opportunities. Tables 6.2 and 6.3 summarise the main
features of Dubai's rapid inward tourism development.

Table 6.2 Profile of Dubai's hotel development, 1982–92

	1982	1990	1991	1992
Number of hotels				
De luxe	11	11	11	12
First class	15	12	12	14
Second class	10	13	15	23
Third class	6	34	97	108
Total	42	70	135	157
Total beds	6,967	9,103	10,956	14,985
Guest nights	347,000	633,000	717,000	944,000

Source: DCTPB, 1993.

Table 6.3 Overall average room occupancy, all grades of hotel (%)

	1982	1990	1991	1992
De luxe	46	70	68	70
First class	47	64	60	60
Second class	38	58	56	47
Third class	50	42	45	36
Average	46	63	63	53.5

Source: DCTPB, 1993.

A profile of Dubai's visitors

The Dubai Commerce and Tourism Promotion Board (DCTPB) commissioned a study of its visitors to understand their characteristics and requirements, and to determine how to position Dubai as a tourist destination in order to increase its share of the market. Profile and attitude surveys were conducted with tourists in the UAE, most of whom were staying in Dubai, with passengers in transit through Dubai International Airport, and with travellers at the airports in London and Frankfurt. Other methodologies included desk research and a survey of industry experts in the UAE and Europe (DCTPB, 1993).

The origins of Dubai's visitors, and the characteristics of the four main groups are summarised in Tables 6.4 and 6.5. Single visitors and family groups from the surrounding Gulf states predominate. Single people from the Gulf tend to visit Dubai at weekends or public holidays, usually staying in deluxe hotels in the city. Most are below 30 years of

Table 6.4 Nationality of visitors to Dubai (thousands, selected countries of origin)

	1982	*1990*	*1991*	*1992*
UAE	17	37	44	56
Other Gulf states	58	123	180	243
Iraq	3	1	0.3	0.9
Iran	4	42	30	43
Other Arab states	1	7	8	11
Pakistan	9	39	41	65
India	25	60	64	94
Japan	7	6	8	19
UK	45	46	54	64
France	5	6	8	10
Germany	10	27	19	28
USA	11	15	39	28
Total visitors	374,400	632,903	716,642	944,350

Source: Internal DCTPB report, July 1993.

Table 6.5 Profiles of main tourist groups

Classification	*Gulf states*			
	Singles	*Families*	*West European*	*Former USSR*
Total visits 1992	125,000	35,000	30,000	15,000
Tourism expenditure (million Dhm, £1 = 5 Dhm approx.)	240	95	310	410
Average age (years)	29	33	44	35
Percentage with accompanying children	0	59	11	7
Length of stay (days)	1.7	6.3	10.4	6.5
Previously visited Dubai (%)	76	88	23	32

Source: DCTPB, 1993.

age, and are frequent visitors. Families from the Gulf states visit during school holidays and stay in deluxe or medium-price city centre hotels, in furnished apartments or with friends. Their interests include shopping, dining and entertainment. Many rent a car and visit friends.

The majority of Western European visitors are couples without children, and stay in deluxe beach hotels, while budget hotels are used by many Scandinavian tourists. Incentive travellers usually stay in the deluxe city hotels, Europeans enjoy relaxing on the beach and taking excursions, especially to the desert, and they like to visit the gold souk, the creek and museum, travelling by taxis or the free hotel buses.

Visitors from the ex-Soviet countries are increasing in number. Their main interest is in buying consumer goods such as electronics and cameras. They generally travel alone and stay in budget beach or town hotels but they do not do much sightseeing outside the city. The best features of Dubai for them are its climate and shopping.

Dubai's tourism sectors

The 1994 Travel Trade manual claims that Dubai is particularly attractive to 'holidaymakers seeking a relaxing break away from the clouds and crowds, or to active tourists looking for a new and exciting experience'. Table 6.6 indicates the range of activities and excursions promoted by travel companies in Dubai.

The range of activities is constantly being expanded. For example, instruction in desert driving techniques was originally provided for locals, but these courses are now popular with visitors. Shopping is a

Table 6.6 Activities and excursions promoted in Dubai

* City tours featuring the creek, old world souks, and traditional wind tower houses
* Cruises by wooden dhow
* Dubai museum, the restored palace of Sheikh Saeed
* Safaris to camel farms and isolated villages
* Wadi bashing in four-wheel drive vehicles
* Sand skiing
* Desert sunsets followed by a traditional Arabic barbecue
* Camel or horse races (no gambling, but raffles for prizes)
* Bird watching – 360 species, many winter migrants
* Hatta Fort and hotel 2 hours drive from city
* Golf, on grass or sand courses
* Sailing, windsurfing and diving
* Shopping in the souks, malls and duty-free outlets

Table 6.7 Traditional souvenirs

Arabic coffee pots
Arab curved daggers (khanjars)
Prayer beads
Soapstone figures
Turquoise, lapis lazuli, malacite items
Silver antique jewellery from Oman, Yemen and UAE
Brass and silver work
Silver and wooden model dhows
Carpets from Iran and elsewhere

---

major feature of visits to Dubai for tourists, particularly those from neighbouring countries, Eastern Europe, Asia, India and the former Soviet Union. There are many modern department stores and shopping malls, and the traditional souks sell a wide range of quality traditional souvenirs (see Table 6.7), carpets, spices, modern consumer durables and electronic goods. The most famous is the gold souk, lined with shops selling bracelets, necklaces, earrings, bullion, coin and bars. The welcome literature which visitors receive on arrival in Dubai explains that while department stores operate on a fixed price basis, traditional shops regard negotiation as a way of life. Tourists are advised to quote back at the shop keeper a figure well below the original asking price.

Organisation of Dubai's tourism industry

When the Dubai National Air Travel Association (DNATA) was founded in the 1960s it was the state's only travel agent and airport operator. With the increasing development of tourism in Dubai, the original operation has been expanded to include an airline, and divided into specialist inbound, outbound and freight businesses, operated commercially and still owned by the royal family. The 1994 Travel Trade manual indicates that there are now also eighteen independent travel companies based in Dubai offering local excursions, and it lists many other businesses catering to tourists needs.

Dubai has one of the world's highest per capita spending on outward travel, because of its importance as a regional management centre, the large number of expatriots, and its prosperity. In recognition of its significance in generating tourist traffic, and because of the easy access it offers to the surrounding area, the British Tourist Authority has plans to open an office in Dubai. As the general sales agent for twenty-six carriers and the region's largest IATA agency, DNATA is a partner in Business Travel International, employs the latest technology, and is a distributor for Gallileo.

Air Emirates

The government of Dubai decided to launch its own airline, Emirates Airlines, because it considered that insufficient capacity through the airport was a potential threat to further development of the state's status as a regional trade centre. Unlike other airlines in the Middle East, Emirates has always had to operate and compete in an open skies policy, and it is required to be profitable. Few companies in Dubai publish their Financial results, but managers say that the airline has been profitable every year except the second, when it had been investing in route expansion.

Emirates was founded in 1985 with two aircraft wet-leased from PIA for the Delhi–Bombay–Karachi route. At that time, said its managers, DNATA had been described as 'an airline without aircraft because it already had sales, data system, ground handling, and engineering expertise'. In the second year of operation, Emirates began to acquire its own fleet.

The airline's business priorities are business-class passengers, cargo and economy passenger traffic, and it sees tourists as an opportunity to fill remaining capacity. Emirates includes a two-day stopover package in the price of their ticket for passengers transiting Dubai on its growing intercontinental network. Emirates philosophy is to offer a high level of personal service – it was the first airline to install seat back video screens in all three classes. In 1993, it took delivery of its thirteenth airbus, the airbus first to be fitted with satellite telephone systems (*Middle East Travel*, October 1993). After negotiating a code-share route to America with United Airlines, Emirates dropped its daily service to Gatwick in favour of two daily flights into Heathrow, where the two companies have adjacent bays and connecting services.

Dubai International Airport

There are five international airports within 100 km of Dubai, with a combined capacity of 12 million passengers. Dubai has most of the traffic, and is the fastest growing in the region, Table 6.8 shows how its

Table 6.8 The build-up of traffic through Dubai airport

	Total aircraft movements	Freight (kgs)	Passengers total	(Including transit)
1961	1,072			
1971	14,638			
1981	59,161			
1990	77,131	144,282,545	5,016,712	(1,749,794)
1991	73,305	140,322,267	4,396,230	(1,063,699)
1992	87,921	186,435,314	5,444,086	(1,378,301)

Source: Dubai International Airport Annual Review, 1992.

traffic has built up. Its key passenger appeals are the ease of access to shopping and business districts, since the airport is located unusually close to the city centre. Other advantages include the quality and range of its duty free outlets and the fast friendly reception for passengers. It is already possible for a passenger to clear immigration, baggage claim and customs in under 12 minutes, but the goal is a '5 minute airport'. Aircraft are serviced rapidly, with a 45 minutes chocks-on, chocks-off turnaround time. This efficiency, together with the open skies policy makes Dubai an attractive stopover point for airlines operating between Europe and the Far East.

A separate Departure Terminal has been provided for Emirates in a two-phase plan which has been developed to cope initially with 8 million, and later with 13 million passengers annually. This will be followed by a Domestic Flights Terminal for traffic to the other Emirates, and an airport hotel within the transit area.

The DCTPB regards the airport as a major sales tool for the Emirate. It provides visitors with their first impressions, and for the large number of transit passengers it is the only way they have of remembering Dubai. The welcome bureau at the airport features literature about local attractions, offers assistance to incoming passengers and distributes material to transiting passengers of sixty international airlines.

The airport is one of the city's most prominent features. Its modern and sophisticated features emphasise Dubai's role as a metropolitan and business centre of importance to neighbouring states. The city has been expanding around the airport, and this is recognised in the new municipal Master Plan which meshes planned transport and other infrastructure developments with the Airport's needs.

In an interview during the preparation of this case study, Mohi-Din Binhendi, Director General of Civil Aviation explained why the Government accords a high priority to the airport.

Dubai's airport is the nerve centre for the economy. When construction began in 1971, everyone wondered why it was so large, but now it serves sixty airlines and 5.4 million travellers a year. This growth has been achieved by a policy of establishing the best facilities for passengers and airlines.

Dubai Airport Duty Free

The Duty Free provides an example of Dubai airport's determined approach to commercially sound improvements. Before redevelopment in 1986, it had been located in a small, drab area and was run by local concessionaires. However, the 2,045 square-metre basement of the Departures building had been underused. It was converted into a modern complex of twenty-four shops operated by the civil aviation department on the model of Shannon airport. The original management brief was to develop customer oriented services, with profitability a low priority to encourage airlines and passengers to pass through Dubai. The Duty Free turnover has increased from $98 million in 1991 to $134 million in 1992, and it now ranks third after Changi and Schiphol. By 1993 it offered the largest stock list in the world and, by monitoring its customer attitudes and the retail markets, its stock lines are constantly reviewed.

In 1987, a small duty-free shop was provided in the arrivals hall, and in 1989, the main retail area was remodelled again. Escalators now lead down from the departure lounge to an elegant shopping mall where separate stores sell alcohol, tobacco, food, gold and jewellery while other shops are show cases for the best local produce (see Table 6.7). Local suppliers were recruited from souk traders by the Duty Free manager, and 70 per cent of merchandise is sourced locally. 20 per cent of revenue is derived from sales of gold, amounting to 2 tonnes in 1992. All staff are trained in courteous selling techniques and are dressed in smart uniforms. 'Thank you' notes are packaged with goods, which are presented in clearly branded plastic carriers prominently displaying Dubai Airport's logo.

The most remarkable feature of the Duty Free Shopping Mall is the Finest Surprise promotion which was launched in November 1989.

Initially one luxury car was displayed for a raffle, but since Summer 1991, two cars have been raffled at same time – 1,000 tickets are sold for each car at Dhs 500 (£100 approximately), and are only available to bona fide passengers departing or transiting the airport. The tickets are sold in just over a week on average. By December 1993, 260 cars had been raffled and three people had won twice! The first cars offered in 1994 were a BMW 850Ci and a Porsche 911 Carrera 2 Tiptronic.

Arabian Adventures

Arabian Adventures (AA) is the branch of Emirates Airlines which promotes inbound tourism. It functions as a wholesaler and provides professional services to overseas incentive houses, Figure 6.4 illustrates its recommended Incentive programme. AA's other clients include convention organisers and tour operators such as Hayes and Jarvis, British Airways and Kuoni (amongst many others). AA has developed rapidly with the widening network of Emirates Airline, its parent company. In 1992 AA served 10,000 visitors, and the forecast for 1993 was 19,000. The company also services other airlines such as British Airways, providing stop over packages for their clients.

AA's other roles are to help overseas travel staff and travel journalists visiting Dubai to familiarise themselves with the destination; to stage road shows promoting the country overseas; and to arrange entry visas for tourists. Visas can only be issued to a local sponsor and were required until 1993 by all Western visitors except for UK citizens. A report to the DCTPB has pointed out that most competing destinations have no visa requirement, and that since some tour operators charge their clients up to 10 per cent of the package price for procuring the visa, this acts as a significant deterrent to the development of Dubai as a tourist destination. The requirement for visas has subsequently been relaxed for those from Germany (and negotiations with other countries were underway as this case study was in preparation).

AA provides a reception service at the airport, and each client receives a welcome pack on arrival. This contains an informative colour map, a welcome letter printed on the client's tour operator's letterhead, and details of their Representative's hours and contact number. Kuoni is the largest operator, and it has sufficient clients to base its own representative in Dubai, but the other companies' clients are looked after by AA staff, wearing Arabian Adventure uniforms. The welcome pack also includes a brochure promoting excursions operated by AA.

DUBAI:
FOR AN
INCENTIVE
WITH A
DIFFERENCE

The rapid growth of incentive travel in recent years has presented organisers with a major challenge. How do you find somewhere new and different that combines variety and excitement with professional destination management services and top quality hotels?

There can be no better answer than "Dubai"— as an increasing number of incentive travel organisers are finding out.

Dubai's unique attraction is that it brings together in a single, accessible location the highest international standards of comfort and convenience with the adventure of traditional Arabia — from the bustling souks to the majestic desert. An exotic destination with a cosmopolitan lifestyle, Dubai has the necessary ingredients to make it the ideal solution for the incentive travel planner.

Dubai is still a sufficiently well kept "secret" to excite the most jaded traveller, yet it offers all the facilities and expertise you need to plan your incentive with confidence.

INCENTIVE PLANNER'S CHECKLIST

Getting There

▶ Dubai's location makes for easy accessibility. London is seven hours away; Frankfurt six; Hong Kong eight; and Nairobi four.
▶ Wide choice of carriers; some 60 airlines provide direct air links to more than 100 cities worldwide.
▶ One of the world's leading inter-continental transit centres, Dubai International Airport is modern and efficient.
▶ Rapid immigration and custom formalities.

Hotels

▶ Wide choice of luxury modern accommodation at competitive prices.
▶ Major international hotel chains well represented— Hyatt Regency, Sheraton, Hilton, Inter-Continental, Ramada, Forte, Marriott and Holiday Inn — as well as independents such as the Royal Abjar.
▶ Top class beach resort hotels — Jebel Ali, Chicago Beach and Metropolitan — and mountain resort at Hatta Fort.
▶ Extensive range of restaurants featuring cuisine from around the world.
▶ Varied nightlife — bars, pubs, night-clubs and discos.
▶ Fully equipped conference and meeting rooms.
▶ Superb health club and sporting facilities including pools and private beaches.

Figure 6.4 Arabian Adventure's incentive programme

Ground Arrangements

▶ Choice of internationally experienced destination management companies and inbound tour operators.
▶ Multi-lingual guides and well qualified drivers.
▶ Modern air-conditioned coaches for airport transfers and excursion tours.
▶ Uncrowded streets, easy parking and wide tree-lined boulevards make getting around a pleasure.

Tours and Excursions

▶ Variety of standard or tailor-made tours available — lasting from one or two hours to several days.
▶ City tours — general, shopping, sightseeing, heritage etc.
▶ Excursions to the desert or through wadis (dried up river beds), to the starkly beautiful Hajar mountains or sandy beaches of the East Coast on the waters of the Indian Ocean.
▶ Visits to neighbouring Emirates provide a variety of attractions, such as the camel market at Al Ain or the dhow building yard in Ajman.
▶ Helicopter, boat and dhow tours.
▶ Special interest packages — golf, watersports, archaeology, etc.

Arabian Adventures

▶ Desert safaris, dune driving and wadi-bashing.
▶ Moonlit Arabian barbecues in the desert, complete with traditional entertainment.
▶ Camel racing and falconry.
▶ Cruises by traditional wooden dhow on the Dubai Creek or into the Gulf.

▶ The exotic sights and sounds of traditional commerce in the bustling souks and on the quays of the Creek.
▶ Photographic opportunities galore — elegant mosques, sumptuous palaces, brightly dressed children, majestic camels, ancient wind-towers, dusty villages and dramatic sunsets.

Outdoor Activities and Sports

▶ Swimming or relaxing by the poolside or by Dubai's miles of clean, uncrowded, sandy beaches.
▶ Superb watersports — sailing, fishing, windsurfing, water-skiing, scuba diving and snorkelling.
▶ Golf in the desert on championship standard grass courses — the famous Emirates Golf Club, the Dubai Creek Golf Club and the Dubai Racing and Golf Club.
▶ Wide range of other sports, from squash and tennis to horseback riding, cycling, ice-skating, shooting, archery and go-karting.
▶ A full calendar of top class international events — rallying, tennis, powerboat racing, football, rugby, volleyball, snooker, showjumping and sailing — makes Dubai the "sports capital of the Middle East".

Shopping

▶ Tax free shopping means bargains galore.
▶ Choice of modern air-conditioned malls or ancient souks.
▶ Wide selection of low priced international brand name products — hi-fi, video, cameras, fashions, watches etc.
▶ Attractive traditional Middle Eastern gifts — coffee pots, rugs, silverware, jewellery, brass, etc.
▶ One of the world's great gold trading centres — unbeatable value.
▶ Award-winning Dubai Duty Free Complex at the airport.

Figure 6.4 *(continued)*

SAMPLE INCENTIVE PROGRAMME

The following sample seven-day incentive programme is designed to provide a taste of the variety and range of new and "different" options that Dubai presents to the incentive planner. It is only an example, and Dubai's tour operators will work with you to develop your own tailor-made programme.

Day 1

Late evening arrival at Dubai International Airport. Bilingual guides escort guests through immigration and baggage reclaim out to luxury air-conditioned coaches. Welcome banner arranged outside the airport.

One person can be sped ahead to the hotel and dressed in Arab national costume to greet the group. A special check-in room will be decorated as a Majlis — a traditional meeting room — and cocktails and canapes will be served as an Arabic band welcomes the guests.

The guests receive a personalised welcome envelope with the itinerary in their native language, a general information sheet on the UAE and a small Persian prayer mat. There is also a gift of a brass coffee pot in each room. The coffee pot is a traditional symbol of Arab hospitality, originating from the days of living in tents when every stranger would be welcomed with a cup of hot coffee.

Day 2

Buffet brunch at hotel poolside.

In the afternoon a fascinating city tour will afford visitors the chance to sample the culture and history of bygone Dubai. Our route takes us to the museum, housed in a 150 year old fort, through the Bastakia district of old wind-towered and mud-walled houses, into the souks of gold, silks and spices, past magnificent palaces and across the Creek on an abra (a water taxi) to gaze on the modern metropolis that is Dubai's centre. Return to hotel at approximately 1830 hours.

Dinner at the Dubai World Trade Club, overlooking the city from a dramatic vantage point on the thirty-third floor of the World Trade Centre, the tallest tower in the Gulf.

Day 3

Following breakfast at the hotel, guests will be escorted to the hotel car park to board helicopters for transfer to the majestic high dunes of Liwa for sand skiing (equipment will be provided). Transfer to hotel for lunch.

Afternoon at leisure. A coach driver and guide available for guests who wish to go shopping.

Guests collected by coach and escorted to a luxury restaurant specialising in traditional Arabic cuisine, followed by a night on the town - at a disco or maybe an Arabian nightclub.

Day 4

Breakfast at poolside. Transferred at 0845 to the Creek for an exciting fishing trip in the Gulf in an Arabian dhow. Guests will be provided with traditional Arabic hand lines.

Catches will be cooked and lunch served on board. Return to hotel around 1430 hours.

Afternoon: shopping trip. The first stop is Karama, famous for its bargains. Then to Al Fahidi Street where the best buys are electronics,

cassette and video tapes and watches. Finally, a short walk into a textile souk with material for both men and women and a host of tailors ready to make your purchases into fashionable clothes.

The evening is spent at one of Dubai's popular restaurants, perhaps specialising in Tex-Mex food, with music from a live band. Late return to hotel.

Day 5

Guests will be taken to the Dubai Camel Race Track for a camel race if scheduled.

Following the race, breakfast will be served in a tent behind the track. Guests then split into two groups. Group 1 will leave for the hotel's private beach club to avail themselves of the beach facilities, while Group 2 will leave for their desert driving course before returning to the beach club for a barbecue lunch.

Group 1 will spend the afternoon at the desert driving course and return to hotel at 1800 hours, while Group 2 spend the afternoon on the beach.

Prior to dinner at the hotel, guests will be presented with their Desert Driving Course Certificates.

Day 6

Morning departure for the Hatta Fort Hotel, at the foot of the Hajar mountains which form the backbone of the Emirates. The journey is spectacular. The sand dunes become taller and turn a beautiful amber-red colour until they merge with the mountains. Among the facilities of the award-winning mountain-lodge-style hotel are archery and clay pigeon shooting, where a "sharpshooter's challenge" has been arranged.

Champagne will be served and lunch will be a banquet in the gardens. There will be plenty of time for a refreshing dip in the pool with piped underwater music.

Mid-afternoon the group leaves in a fleet of powerful four-wheel-drive vehicles. After some spectacular dune-driving, the cars emerge over a dune to find a champagne bar lit by the setting sun. Nearby is a Bedouin camp. Everyone is given traditional Arab dress for the grand celebration. A local band alternates with western music. The goat hair tents are set out with low tables and full silver service.

After dinner, the sound of hooves is heard. The lights swing and three camels come into view. The middle camel carries only a rolled up Persian carpet. The riders of the two others present the carpet to a member of the group as a token of appreciation from the Sheikhs. Ceremoniously, the Bedouins present a traditional dagger or "Khanjar" to cut the string binding the carpet. The carpet unravels across the sand to reveal a beautiful belly dancer. A perfect end to the evening.

Departure back to hotel at approximately 2200 hours.

Day 7

Breakfast at the hotel. Baggage transferred to airport for check-in formalities.

Guests transferred to the airport for return flight, giving ample time for last minute shopping at the famous Dubai Duty Free Shopping Complex.

Figure 6.4 *(continued)*

A manager explained that the philosophy behind the programme is to 'offer visitors activities which give them the flavour of Arabia, while they stay in hotels which offer the comfort of Europe'.

Dubai's hotels

In 1993, Dubai had 8,214 hotel rooms in 157 hotels, twenty-six of which are regarded as suitable for Western tourists. Sheraton, Hilton and the Inter-Continental feature amongst the international chains with properties in the city, while Holiday Inn, Trust House Forte and Marriott had properties under construction. Profiles of these new properties are given in Table 6.9.

One of Dubai's most successful established hotels, the Metropolitan, is located near the new Holiday Inn Crowne Plaza. The Metropolitan is owned and operated by the Al Habtoor group, which has diversified holdings including engineering, construction, car sales (it is the agent for Rolls Royce, Aston Martin, and Mitsubishi), catering, real estate and education, in addition to its hotel interests.

The Metropolitan opened in 1979 with 200 rooms. In anticipation of the increased competition likely to result from the opening of several major new hotels in Dubai, the Metropolitan has undergone an extensive refurbishment programme and has adopted a number of service enhancements. One floor is now dedicated to 'butler service', the first available in the Gulf area. The butler will unpack suitcases, deliver morning coffee, and arrange concert tickets. The hotel management explained the other advantages of the concept for business visitors.

Table 6.9 Profile of hotels under construction, 1993

Marriott

235 rooms, part of a complex with 3 levels of shops, 35 food outlets, 1,000 car spaces and office accommodation

Forte Grand Jumeria Beach

247 room 10 storey hotel, Royal suite, 3 superior suites 27 Tower suites and 21 Royal club rooms

Holiday Inn Crowne Plaza

406 rooms, banquet facilities, high-tech conference equipment, a commercial tower, a two storey shopping mall and a 226 apartment block

Source: Dubai Update, various editions.

Guests will only deal with one person during their entire stay at the hotel. Requests will be carried out by the person asked to. Professionally trained butlers are being recruited internationally. Repeat visitors will be assigned the same butler, who will get to know guests individually.

A notable feature of the hotel is the twelve high standard catering outlets, including those specialising in Indian, Chinese and Italian cuisine. It also offers a coffee shop and a choice of bars and a night club. The Metropolitan is situated on the main road leading to Abu Dhabi, close to the Jebel Ali Free Trade Zone and its catering and entertainment facilities are popular with the professional and managerial expatriot residents of the surrounding area.

The Metropolitan attracts both long and short stay corporate clients, while its sister property, located on a private beach, is popular with tour operators from Western Europe. Guests of either hotel are able to enjoy the amenities of the other, with a courtesy coach shuttling between them and to the city centre. Both properties provide facilities for guests at Dubai's three grass golf courses, and they are linked to an international golf organisation providing accommodation packages which include a complimentary round of golf with each night's accommodation.

The Metropolitan Beach Resort has ninety rooms, and sixteen junior suites. Its guests have a choice of five restaurants, and a range of leisure amenities. These include tennis and squash courts, a gym and sauna. In addition to its large, clean private beach the resort has a children's pool, and a swim-in bar in the Olympic size pool which is cooled during the summer months.

This hotel too has been upgraded ahead of the planned reconstruction of one its main competitors, the Chicago Beach hotel and the opening of the Trust House Forte Jumeria beach hotel. As well as a small luxury hotel, the Metropolitan Beach is an exclusive private club, but during remodelling, the Metropolitan's security gate was relocated inside the compound to encourage passing traffic to use the resort's restaurant facilities. However, only club members, and guests registered at either of the two Metropolitan hotels, can gain access to its leisure amenities and the beach, thus ensuring an exclusive and relaxed atmosphere. The uncrowded beach will be a major asset to the Metropolitan's hotel business, because under a recent change in legislation all future properties must provide free public access to their beach.

Virtually all Dubai's hotels are located in the city, or along the nearby beaches. The Hatta Fort Hotel is a notable exception. It offers fifty-four luxury individual chalet-style rooms, and is located in an extensive oasis set in the starkly beautiful Hajar mountains, an hour's drive from the city. The grounds are landscaped, and provide a range of activities for guests including a free-form swimming pool, Olympic target and field archery, clay pigeon shooting, floodlit tennis, mini-golf, walking and jogging routes. Four-wheel drive excursions are organised for guests in the surrounding area.

The development of Dubai's tourism

The development of visitor attractions

The City of Dubai has an objective of becoming a modern city which, although developing rapidly, values its traditions and culture, and provides a safe, pleasant and verdant environment. Table 6.10 shows the range of projects announced or in progress during late 1993 intended to benefit visitors and to enhance the enjoyment of residents.

Dubai claims that it has the best range of golf facilities in the Gulf with three grass courses in contrasting styles. Each is government-backed as part of the overall plan to promote Dubai as a centre for business and trade, and a place where international companies want to come and do business.

The Desert Classic is held annually at the Emirates Golf Club, and as the opening event on the European PG professional golf tour, it attracts considerable international attention. Dubai Creek Golf and Yacht Club was opened in 1993. Its membership has been restricted to 200 in order to provide ample access for visitors. The Club is located off the main highway linking the city and the airport. It has an eighteen-hole championship grass course, floodlit par 3, 4 and 5 practice holes, and an impressive clubhouse whose architecture reflects the theme of traditional Arab dhow sails. The club house has a five-star restaurant, coffee shop, bars and function facilities, a Pro-shop, gym, and a swimming pool.

During construction of the course, 450,000 cubic metres of earth were shifted the greens and grounds require up to 4.5 million litres of desalinated water a day in the summer. This is piped in from the aluminium smelter, stored in three irrigation lakes holding 72 million litres and used to irrigate the grounds at night. One result has been a notable

Table 6.10 Developments to Dubai's tourism facilities, 1993

---

* Restoration of a traditional school
  to exhibit the role of education in the UAE with photos, and to show local
  traditional architecture

* Beautification of the creek side
  and provision of paths and walkways with specialist gardens including a traditional
  date farm

* A new marina complex and world-class golf club
  a few minutes drive from the airport and city centre

* Extension of the fort which houses the Dubai Museum
  maintaining its character by constructing underground

* Development of a 500-hectare park
  on the Sharja border featuring a beach, green area, swimming for children, internal
  transport, catering, shade, outside parking

* Conversion of Sheikh Saeed Al Maktoum House
  into a museum displaying documents and photos of UAE and Dubai's history

* Safa Park improvements
  including sports, lake with fountain, local, European and Oriental gardens

* Construction of a tourist village in the desert
  the first in the Gulf, its design will reflect 'ancient Dubai', where visitors can
  participate in traditional pastimes

Source: Dubai Update, various editions.

increase in the number and variety of birds in the area. An exclusive yacht club and marina is located nearby, on the Creek itself. A recreational park is being created on the opposite shore of the Creek. This will feature a traditional palm tree farm, watered by underground irrigation channels, operated by modern pumps rather than the traditional water wheels. Buildings in the park are being constructed in the traditional way of handmade mud and stone walls, their roofs are made of palm tree trunks covered with branches and woven palm fronds, and the farm house will function as a traditional coffee shop.

A manager explained the philosophy which underlies these developments: 'The complex presents a strong message from the government to the international business, travel and sporting communities that Dubai has the imagination, the will power and the ability to match, even surpass, the best in the world.'

Informing visitors about Dubai's culture

> Two complementary objectives guide the development of Dubai's
> tourism: to give people what they want, but only attract who we want.
> Word of mouth recommendation and repeat business has been the
> basis of tourism demand, but we are looking for growth. This will be
> achieved by a restrained and classy promotional style evoking tradi-
> tional Arab images of desert life and the modernity of Dubai City.
> Prices will take care of the market profile, as packages are based in
> luxury hotels and beach properties.
>
> (Interview with a senior tourism official)

Although Dubai has a very tolerant attitude to its overseas residents
and to tourists, it is an Islamic state. Foreigners are required to
reciprocate by respecting the religious customs of the Arab nationals.
The state's promotional literature and tour operators' brochures make
clear what is expected, adopting a relaxed style similar in tone to the
advice offered about the climate. For example, one leaflet advises
potential visitors that 'Dubai has a sub tropical, arid climate with
infrequent rainfall averaging only 13 cm a year. Temperatures range
from 10 to 48 degrees centigrade.' A subsequent paragraph states,
'Alcohol is freely available in hotel restaurants and bars, but not outside
the hotels.'

British Airways Holidays 1994 brochure features the Chicago Beach
hotel, or an eight-day tour including the Metropolitan Beach Hotel and
the Hatta Fort. The format of the brochure is to provide advice about
each destination in tinted boxes at the head of each section. The page
featuring Dubai states:

> Dubai is a Moslem country and dress, outside the hotels, should be
> discreet. During the month of Ramadan (in 1994 this should be from
> mid February to mid March depending on the moon), visitors are
> required to refrain from eating, drinking or smoking in public places
> and city restaurants may not be open between sunrise and sunset.
> The standard of cuisine in hotels is high and the choice varied.
> Alcohol is freely available in hotels but not outside.

The Dubai Commerce and Tourism Promotion Board (DCTPB)

The DCTPB was established in 1989. Patrick Macdonald, the Deputy
Chief Executive described its purposes as:

To support the government in ensuring a stable, long term growth of Dubai by promoting economic diversification away from oil and gas. Our focus is to stimulate increased investment in manufacturing, trade, transport and service industries and to develop Dubai as a tourism destination.

He explained that during its first few years of operation, the DCTPB has addressed four tasks.

1 *Product development* – to enhance Dubai as a business and tourist centre by minimising problems for investors, businessmen and visitors.
2 *Promotion* – to plan and implement an annual programme of events, and co-ordinate trade fairs, sporting and cultural events.
3 *Publicity* – to develop Dubai's message and disseminate it to world-wide target audience in the form of media releases, advertising, video, direct mail, information kits, speeches and publications.
4 *Overseas representation* – to appoint local representatives in London, Paris, Milan, Frankfurt, Hong Kong, Tokyo and Philadelphia.

The DCTPB initially received large subsidies for its activities because there had been no tradition of paying for such services in Dubai's tax free environment. It has now been able to demonstrate the effectiveness of its programmes, and increasingly it charges for services on a cost recovery basis.

The DCTPB produced three brochures for travel trade use in 1993/94. 'Dubai, The Watersports Resort' ; 'Dubai, The Classic Golf Destination' and 'Dubai, the Classic Golf Destination.' A fourth brochure promoting the advantages of Dubai as an incentive destination is illustrated in Figure 6.3.

Patrick Macdonald emphasised that tourism in Dubai has to be seen in the context of its role as a commercial centre for the region. This is demonstrated in the way the state promotes itself to the international community. A feature of Dubai's promotional strategy is to secure sponsorship of high profile sports events which appeal to the international business community and attract the attention of potential overseas tourists. Ten international sports events include snooker, tennis, golf, car rallies, karting and power boat racing were staged in Dubai between June and December 1993. The *Gulf News* (30 December 1993) reported that the Dubai Tennis Open was to be staged in early 1994. Its sponsors were to include Duty Free, BMW, the National Bank of Dubai,

Hyatt Regency, Mild Seven, Yashica, *Gulf News*, Dugas, Pepsi, Forte Grand Dubai, and other companies.

Nineteen conferences and exhibitions were hosted in the second half of 1993. One, the 1993 International Aerospace Exhibition attracted 25,000 industry visitors and 400 international journalists. Prince Charles attended the exhibition, which featured 450 exhibitors from 33 nations.

Western Europe – market potential

The winter sun market is one of the main segments of European tour operators' business, attracting nearly 5 million clients. In 1992, 15,000 Western European tourists visited Dubai during the winter, mainly on tour operators' packages. On the basis of its cost, distance and range of attractions, the DCTPB estimates that almost one million Europeans could be considered potential visitors to Dubai. The Deputy Chief Executive of DCTPB remarked that 'our promotional efforts aimed at those one million will be more effective than if we try to reach all 233 million Europeans!'

Almost all European holidaymakers to Dubai purchase inclusive tours, and Kuoni is the leading operator to Dubai from Europe. A report commissioned by the DCTPB included a competitive analysis of the 1992/93 Kuoni brochure. It offered a total of almost 65,000 rooms, 75 per cent of which were costed within 10 per cent of Dubai's price range. Table 6.11 provides a breakdown of the spatial distribution of Kuoni's winter product.

Table 6.11 Geographical distribution of Kuoni's rooms (Winter, 1992/93)

29,820	in Far East
10,766	in Caribbean
2,900	in Kenya coast
4,969	in Egypt
16,000	elsewhere
1,020	in Dubai

Source: DCTPB, 1993.

Development of the German market

The figures cited previously indicate the potential for market development, and Dubai undertakes active product development and promotion, often in conjunction with Emirates Airlines. For example, although Germany is regarded as the best source to develop, there had been no excursion fare while the route was operated only by Lüfthansa. After Emirates established operations to Frankfurt, the two airlines set a joint excursion fare which was comparable to that for Tenerife, thus enabling holiday packages to Dubai from Germany to be priced competitively.

Visa requirements for German citizens were subsequently relaxed, and German citizens are now granted one- or two-year multiple entry visas to enter the UAE for up to three months per year without a sponsor. The visas are free of charge by the UAE embassy in Germany (*Dubai Travel and Tourism News*, October 1993).

Thirty-eight German tour operators offered packages to Dubai in 1993/94, an increase of 25 per cent over the preceding year. They include the top five companies in terms of volume, as well as specialists offering golf, diving, nature study, adventure and archaeology tours. More than twenty companies feature summer tours, confirming Dubai's emerging status as a year-round destination. Dubai's success in Germany has resulted from participation in trade fairs, seminars and workshops, media relations, advertising and the production and distribution of brochures in the German language. In addition, DCTPB's German bureau has also recruited thirteen Swiss and Austrian operators who now offer Dubai as a holiday destination.

Marketing Dubai in Britain

Raitt Orr represents the Dubai Commerce and Tourism Promotion Board in Britain and Ireland. Ian Raitt, its director, explained that the London branch was established in 1989, simultaneously with six others around the world to fulfil the four objectives of the newly established DCTPB. (The ensuing section is based on an interview with Ian Raitt conducted in January 1994.)

There were 64,000 visits to Dubai from Britain in 1992. The UK is seen as a strong market for inward investment into Dubai's non-oil economy due to the historical links between the two countries. Several opportunities for the development of the tourism market from Britain follow from our strong business connections. We can expand on the large numbers of business travellers and those attending conferences or exhibitions, by bolting on vacation packages for a spouse, or developing special interest tours for ornithologists, archaeologists and so on. Another important benefit is the personal endorsement of Dubai as a holiday destination by business visitors who know the area well.

We disseminate Dubai's messages to key audiences in several ways. Dubai does not undertake consumer advertising, instead we provide facilities for influential journalists to visit the state. During the last year, we have assisted ten journalists from titles as diverse as *Horse and Hound, Meeting and Incentive Travel, Business Traveller* and the BBC *Top Gear* and *Travel Show* programmes.

Another strand to our service is a monthly 'Dubai Update.' This is a compilation of articles culled from media sources in the Gulf. The demand for this has built up from about twenty to nearly 2,000. One reason for its success is that we get it to our readers just before the beginning of each month, so it is very up-to-date. It features short articles of general interest, and others of concern to investors, politicians, the business community, journalists and travel retailers and tour operators.

The London office works with business oriented organisations such as Chambers of Commerce in Britain and Ireland. We stage seminars for them which typically consist of an introduction by one of our directors or executives, and a talk on a topic relevant to the particular audience either by a prominent UK business leader or an official from Dubai. This is followed by a film about the business opportunities of the area, which also explains how to set up a joint venture there. Our message is that Dubai is the ideal centre in the Middle East for distribution. Its location gives it the potential to service countries from Arabia to Eastern China, and from East Africa to the newly independent countries of Central Asia. The facilities which Dubai has for import–export and warehousing are ideal for the 'just in time' approach to business in the area.

A key factor in the development of the UK holiday market to Dubai is the excellent air connections between them. In January 1994, seven airlines provided direct flights, including a double daily service from Heathrow by Emirates and a daily British Airways flight. Several consolidators provided fares ranging from £375 return, and lower fares were available on connecting services through European or Middle Eastern centres.

We arrange presentations for travel professionals to inform them of Dubai's facilities and attractions. Often, these are staged jointly with one of the airlines which feature Dubai as a destination. We also organise Dubai's representation at major events such as World Travel Market (WTM). In 1992, Dubai was awarded the prize for the best stand. The 1993 show featured 5,500 organisations from 137 countries, and Dubai was represented by the DCTPB, Dept of Civil Aviation, Dubai Duty Free, Emirates, three golf clubs, three tour operators and thirteen leading hotels. Dubai's stand was again highly visible in trade and consumer media coverage. During WTM, Dubai was featured in ten trade journals, and the editorial coverage we obtained in these alone would have cost about £24,000 if we had bought the space. This is significant because our strategy is to create travel industry awareness.

As well as informing travel retailers about Dubai, we encourage tour operators to develop packages to Dubai. We highlight the success of Dubai as a destination, emphasising that its unique combination of features has resulted in good business for all operators who feature it. We can help them by setting up links with Arabian Adventures or other GHAs (Ground Handling Agents).

One of our advantages is that this marketing agency [Raitt Orr] is known for its work in representing a variety of international clients, and this experience gives objectivity and credibility when we recommend Dubai's specific attributes as a business centre or as a travel destination.

In 1990, only Kuoni, Jasmin and Swan Hellenic had tours from the UK to Dubai. By January 1994 nineteen tour operators featured Dubai as a single destination, a stopover or in multiple destination combination tours. Prices ranged from £369 for a three-night package up to £2,700 for a special interest fifteen-day tour of the Emirates. A typical price for a seven-night beach hotel package was about £700.

Suggested exercises

1 Identify the elements, subsystems and stakeholders in Dubai's tourism. Do you consider that the systems modelling approach is helpful in understanding the development, effects and role of tourism in Dubai?
2 Evaluate the steps being taken to expand and control tourism in Dubai.

3 Examine the imagery employed in current tour operators' brochures for Dubai and competing destinations. Discuss your findings.

4 Using the information supplied in this chapter, conduct a marketing audit and SWOT analysis of the tourism industry in Dubai.

5 What research do you recommend that Dubai should carry out in the markets where its tourism business originates, beyond that outlined in this case study?

6 'Dubai has no formal tourism plan.' Contrast the approach adopted by Dubai to ensure the future of its tourism industry with that of other countries.

References and select bibliography

Akehurst, G., Bland, N. and Nevin, M. (1994) 'Successful tourism policies in the European Union', *Journal of Vacation Marketing* 1, 1: 11–27.

Allen, L. R., Hafer, H. R., Long, P. T. and Perdue, R. R. (1993) 'Rural residents' attitudes towards recreation and tourism development', *Journal of Travel Research* Spring, 27–33.

Ansoff, H. I. (1968) *Corporate Strategy*, London: Penguin.

Ashworth, G. and Goodall, B. (1991) *Marketing Tourism Places*, London: Routledge.

Ashworth G. and Voogd, H. (1990) 'Can places be sold for tourism?', in G. Ashworth and B. Goodall (eds) *Marketing Tourism Places*, London: Routledge.

Asseal, H. (1987) *Consumer Behavior And Marketing Action*, Boston: Kent Publishers.

Baker, J. (1994) *Channel '94, Evaluation Research*, Tunbridge Wells: SEETB.

Baker, M. (1989) *Tourism for All*, London: English Tourist Board.

Baum, T. (ed.) (1993) *Human Resource Issues in International Tourism*, Oxford: Butterworth Heinemann.

Beck, P. (1994) 'Managing Antarctic tourism', *Annals of Tourism Research* April, 375–86.

Bell, G. (1907) *The Desert and the Sown*, republished by Virago, London, 1985.

Berry, T. H. (1991) *Managing the Total Quality Transformation*, New York: McGraw-Hill.

Bodlender, J. (1991) 'Planning in action', in L. J. Lickorish (ed.) *Developing Tourism Destinations, Policies and Perspectives*, Harlow: Longman.

Bodlender J. A. and Ward T. J. (1989) 'Profile of investment incentives', in

S. F. Witt and L. Moutinho (eds) *Tourism Marketing and Management Handbook*, London: Prentice Hall.

Boorstin, D. (1975) *The Image, A Guide to Psuedo-events in America*, New York: Atheneum.

Bramwell, B. (1991) 'UK theme parks in the 1990's', *Tourism Management* March, 78–9.

Brown, F. (1991) 'Tourism for all', conference report, *Tourism Management* September

BTA (British Tourist Authority) (1985) *An Opportunity for the Nation*, London: BTA.

Buck, E. (1993) *Paradise Remade, The Politics of Culture and History in Hawai'i*, Philadelphia: Temple University Press.

Budowski, G. (1976) 'Tourism and conservation, conflict, coexistence and symbiosis', *Environmental Conservation* 3, 27–31.

Bull, A. (1991) *The Economics of Travel and Tourism*, Melbourne: Pitman.

Butler, R. (1993) 'Pre and post impact assessment of tourism development', in D. Pearce and R. Butler (eds) *Tourism Research, Critiques and Challenges*, London: Routledge.

Carver, G. (1993) 'Regional marketing in a European context', *Tourism Bulletin* October, 10–11.

Checkland, P. and Scholes, J. (1990) *Soft Systems Methodology in Action*, Chichester: John Wiley.

Chisnall, P. M. (1985) *Marketing, A Behavioural Analysis*, London: McGraw-Hill.

Cohen, E. (1972) 'Towards a sociology of international tourism', *Social Research* 39, 1: 164–82.

Cohen, J. B. (1968) 'Involvement, separating the state from its causes and effects', quoted in W. L. Wilkie (ed.), *Consumer Behaviour*, Chichester: John Wiley.

Coleman, C. (1992) *Customer Care*, Consultative Paper No 8, Cardiff: Wales Tourist Board.

Cooper, C. and Latham, J. (1994) 'Tourism 1992', *Leisure Management* January, 24, 25.

Cooper, C., Fletcher, J., Gilbert, D. and Wanhill, S. (1993) *Tourism, Principles and Practice*, London: Pitman.

Cowell, D. (1986) *The Marketing Of Services*, London: Heinemann.

Crouch, S. (1985) *Marketing Research For Managers*, London: Pan.

CSO (Central Statistical Office) (1994) *Annual Abstract of Statistics*, London: HMSO.

D'Amore, L. (1983) 'Guidelines to planning in harmony with the host community', in P. Murphy (ed.) *Tourism Canada, Selected Issues and Options*.

Darnell, A., Johnson, P. and Thomas, B. (1992) 'Modelling visitor flows at the Beamish Museum', in P. Johnson and B. Thomas (eds) *Choice and Demand in Tourism*, London: Mansell.

Davis, H. L. (1976) 'Decision making within the household', *Journal of Consumer Research* March, 2: 241–60.

DCTPB (1993) *Dubai Tourism Survey, 1992/93*, Dubai: Dryland Consultants.

De Kadt, T. (1979) *Tourism, Passport To Development*, Oxford and New York: Oxford University Press.

Defert, P. (1967) *Le Taux de Fonction touristique: mise au point et critique*, Aix-en-Provence: Centre des Hautes Etudes Touristiques. Cited in S. L. J. Smith (ed.) (1989) *Tourism Analysis, A Handbook*, Harlow: Longman.

Doxey, G. U. (1975) 'A causation theory of visitor–resident irritants, methodology and research inferences', *Proceedings of the Travel and Tourism Research Association Proceedings*.

Edington, J. M. and Edington, M. A. (1990) *Ecology, Recreation and Tourism*, Cambridge: Cambridge University Press.

Embacher, E. and Buttle, F. (1989) 'A repertory grid analysis of Austria's image as a summer vacation destination', *Journal of Travel Research* Winter, 3–7.

Engel, J. F., Blackwell, R. D. and Miniard, P. W. (1986) *Consumer Behavior*, Chicago: Dryden Press.

Enzenbacher, D. (1993) 'Tourists in Antarctica, numbers and trends', *Tourism Management* April, 142–6.

ETB (English Tourist Board) (1985) *Holiday Motivations*, London: ETB.

Featherstone M. (1982) 'The body in consumer culture', *Theory, Culture and Society* 1: 18–33.

Fishbein, M. and Ajzen, I. (1975) *Belief, Attitudes, Intentions And Behaviour*, Reading, MA: Addison-Wesley.

Fodness, D. (1992) 'The impact of family life cycle on the vacation decision making process', *Journal of Travel Research* Autumn, 8–13.

Fontayne, C. (1991) 'Capturing and communicating image'. *Proceedings of the Travel and Tourism Research Association*, 355–7.

Garvin, D. A. (1988) *Managing Quality*, New York: Free Press.

Goffman, E. (1959) *The Presentation of Self In Everyday Life*, New York: Doubleday.

Goodall, B. and Bergsma, J. (1990) 'Destinations as marketed in tour operators' brochures', in G. Ashworth and B. Goodall (eds) *Marketing Tourism Places*, London: Routledge.

Goodenough, R. (1992) 'The use of environmental impact assessment in the management of open space and recreational land in California', *International Journal of Environmental Studies* 40, 171–84.

Grover, R. (1991) *The Disney Touch*, Irwin, IL: Business One.

Gummesson, E. (1988) 'Service quality and product quality combined', *Review of Business* 9, 3: 14–19.

Gunn, C. A. (1988a) *Vacationscape, Designing Tourist Regions*, New York: Van Nostrand Reinhold.

—— (1988b) *Tourism Planning*, New York: Taylor & Francis.

Hall, C. (1992) *Hallmark Tourist Events, Impacts, Management, Planning,*

London: Belhaven Press.

Hall, C. and McArthur, C. (1993) 'Ecotourism in Antarctica', *Tourism Management* Spring, 117–22.

Hawkins, D. (1993) 'Global assessment of tourism policy', in D. Pearce and R. Butler (eds) *Tourism Research, Critiques and Challenges*, London: Routledge.

Heggenhougen, H. (1987) 'Traditional medicine (in developing countries): intrinsic value and relevance for holistic health care, *Holistic Medicine* 2 47–56.

Holder, J. S. (1992) 'The need for public–private sector cooperation in tourism', *Tourism Management* June, 157–62.

Holloway, J. C. (1994) *The Business of Tourism*, 4th edn, London: Pitman.

Holloway, J. C. and Plant, R. V. (1992) *Marketing For Tourism*, London: Pitman.

Horivitz, J. and Panak, M. J. (1992) *Total Customer Satisfaction, Lessons From 50 European Companies With Top Quality Services*, London: Pitman.

Inskeep, E. (1993) *National and Regional Planning, Methodologies and Case Studies*, Madrid: WTO.

Inskeep, E. and Kallenberger, M. (1992) *An Integrated Approach To Resort Development*, Madrid: WTO.

Jansen-Verbeke, M. (1991) 'Leisure shopping, a magic concept for the tourism industry?', *Tourism Management* March, 9–14.

Jeffries, D. (1989) 'Selling Britain, a case for privatisation, *Travel and Tourism Analyst* Spring, 69–81.

Jenner, P. and Smith, C. (1993) *Tourism in the Mediterranean*, London: EIU Research Report.

Jubenville, A., Twight, D. W. and Becker, R. H. (1987) *Outdoor Recreation Management Theory And Applications*, State College, PA: Venture Publishing.

Kay, S. (1987) *Land of the Emirates*, Dubai: Motivate Publishing.

Kelly, J. R. (1990) *Leisure*, Englewood Cliffs, NJ: Prentice-Hall.

King, B. and Whitelaw, P. (1992) 'Resorts in Australian tourism', *Journal of Tourism Studies* December, 41–9.

Kotler, P. H. (1982) *Principles of Marketing*, Englewood Cliffs, NJ: Prentice-Hall.

—— (1984) *Marketing Management, Analysis, Planning And Control*, Englewood Cliffs, New Jersey: Prentice-Hall.

Kotler, P., Haider, D. H. and Rein, I. (1993) *Marketing Places*, New York: Free Press.

Krippendorf, J. (1987) *The Holiday Makers*, London: Heinemann.

Law, C. M. (1993) *Urban Tourism, Attracting Visitors to Large Cities*, London: Mansell.

Laws, E. (1986) 'Identifying and managing the consumerist gap', *Service Industries Journal* July, 131–43.

—— (1991) *Tourism Marketing, Service and Quality Management Perspectives*, Cheltenham: Stanley Thornes.

—— (1992) 'Service analysis – a consumerist gap taxonomy', *Service Industries Journal* January, 116–24.

—— (1994) 'The Delphic oracle – forecasting the future for British tourism', *Tourism* March, 131–43.

—— (forthcoming) *The Holiday Industry*, London: Routledge.

Lea, J. (1988) *Tourism and Development in the Third World*, London: Routledge.

Leiper, N. (1990) *Tourism Systems*, Palmerston North, New Zealand: Massey University Press.

Leppard, J. and McDonald, M. (1987) 'A reappraisal of the role of marketing planning', *Journal of Marketing Research*. Winter.

Levitt, T. (1969) *The Marketing Mode*, New York: McGraw-Hill.

Lickorish, L. (1991a) 'Developing a single European tourism policy', *Tourism Management* September, 178–84.

—— (1991b) *Developing Tourism Destinations, Policies and Perspectives*, Harlow: Longman.

Lim, N. Z. (1993) 'Planning for sustainable tourism, the Philippine experience', *Round Table on Planning For Sustainable Tourism Development*, conference report, Bali: WTO.

Lockwood, A. (1989) 'Quality management in hotels', in S. F. Witt and L. Moutinho (eds) *Tourism Marketing and Management Handbook*, London: Prentice-Hall. London: 1989.

Lockyer, K. G. and Oakland J. S. (1981) 'How to sample success', *Management Today*. July.

Ma Ruilin (1992) 'Goose, or golden egg?', *China Now*. Winter: 19.

MacCannell, D. (1976) *The Tourist, A New Theory Of The Leisure Class*, London: Macmillan Press.

—— (1992) *Empty Meeting Grounds*, London: Routledge.

Machlis, G. and Field, D. (eds) (1992) *On Interpretation, Sociology for Interpreters of Natural and Cultural History*, Corvallis, OR: Oregn State University Press.

Martin, B. and Mason, S. (1993) 'The future for attractions', *Tourism Management* February, 35–40.

Mayo, E. and Jarvis, L. (1981) *The Psychology of Leisure Travel*, Boston, MA: CBI.

Middleton, V. T. C. (1988) *Marketing In Travel and Tourism*, Oxford: Heinemann.

Mill, R. C. and Morrison, A. M. (1985) *The Tourism System*, Englewood Cliffs, NJ: Prentice-Hall.

Misra, S. K. (1993), 'Heritage preservation in sustainable tourism development'. *Round Table on Planning for Sustainable Tourism Development*, conference report, Bali: WTO.

Moeller, G. H. and Shaffer, E. L. (1987) 'The Delphi technique, a tool for long range tourism and travel planning', in J. R. Brent Ritchie and C. R. Goeldner (eds) *Travel, Tourism and Hospitality Research*, New York: Wiley.

Morgan, M. (1991) 'Dressing up to survive: marketing Majorca anew'. *Tourism Management* March, 15–20.

Morgan M. (1994) 'Homogenous products: the future of established resorts', in W. Theobald (ed.) *Global Tourism, The Next Decade*, Oxford: Butterworth Heinemann.

Murphy, P. (1985) *Tourism, A Community Approach*, London: Methuen.

NEDO (1992a) *Marketing the UK Holiday in the UK*, London: NEDO/Tourism Society.

—— (1992b) *UK Tourism, Competing For Growth*, London: NEDO/Tourism Society.

Normann, R. (1991) *Service Management, Strategy And Leadership In Service Businesses*, Chichester: John Wiley.

OECD (1981) *Case Studies Of The Impact Of Tourism On The Environment*, Paris: OECD.

Paddison, R. (1983) *The Fragmented State And The Political Geography Of Power*, Oxford: Blackwell.

Page, S. J. (1992) 'Perspectives on tourism and peripherality: a review of tourism in the Republic of Ireland', in C. Cooper (ed.) *Progress in Tourism, Recreation and Hospitality Management*, London: Belhaven Press.

Parasuraman, A., Zeithmal, V. A. and Berry, L. L. (1988) 'SERVQUAL: multiple item for measuring consumer perceptions of service quality', *Journal of Retailing* Spring, 12–40.

Pearce, D. (1980) 'Tourism and regional development, a genetic approach', *Annals of Tourism Research* 7, 1: 69–82.

—— (1989) *Tourist Development*, Harlow: Longman Scientific.

—— (1992) *Tourist Organizations*, Harlow: Longman.

Pearce, D. and Butler, R. (eds) (1993) *Tourism Research, Critiques and Challenges*, London: Routledge.

Pearce, P. L. (1988) *The Ulysses Factor, Evaluating Visitors in Tourist Settings*, New York: Springer-Verlag.

Picard, M. (1991) 'Cultural tourism in Bali', paper presented at ASEAUK Conference, Hull.

Pigram, J. (1990) 'Sustainable tourism – policy considerations'. *Annals of Tourism Research* 1, 2:, 3–9.

Pi-Sunyer, O. (1989) 'Changing perceptions of tourism and tourists in a Catalan resort town', in V. Smith (ed.) *Hosts and Guests*, Philadelphia: University of Pennsylvania Press.

Radburn, M. and Goodall, B. (1990) 'Marketing through travel agents', in G. Ashworth and B. Goodall (eds) *Marketing Tourism Places*, London: Routledge.

Reynolds, P. (1993) 'Food and tourism, towards an understanding of sustainable tourism', *Journal of Sustainable Tourism* 1, 1: 48–54.

Richardson, J. and Cohen, J. (1993) 'State slogans, the case of the missing USP',

Journal of Travel and Tourism Marketing 2, 2/3: 91–109.

Richter, L. K. (1989) *The Politics of Tourism in Asia*, Honolulu: University of Hawaii Press.

Ritchie, J. R. and Zins, M. (1978) 'Culture as a determinant of the attractiveness of a tourist region', *Annals of Tourism Research* 5: 252–67.

Romeril, M. (1989) 'Tourism, the environmental dimension', in C. Cooper (ed.) *Progress in Tourism, Recreation and Hospitality Management*, London: Belhaven Press.

Ryan, C. (1991) *Recreational Tourism, A Social Science Perspective*, London: Routledge.

Shaw, G. and Williams, A. (1987) 'Formation and operating characteristics in the Cornish tourism industry', *Tourism Management* December, 343–8.

Sheldon, P. and Var, T. (1984) 'Residents' attitudes to tourism in Wales', *Tourism Management* January, 40–7.

Smith, S. L. J. (1983) *Recreation Geography*, Harlow: Longman.

Smith, V. (ed.) (1989) *Hosts and Guests, The Anthropology of Tourism*, 2nd edition, Philadelphia: University of Pennsylvania Press.

Soane, J. V. N. (1993) *Fashionable Resort Regions, Their Evolution and Transformation*, Wallingford: CAB International.

Stabler, M. (1990) 'The concept of opportunity sets as a methodology for selling tourism places', in G. Ashworth and B. Goodall (eds) *Marketing Tourism Places*, London: Routledge.

Tabata, R. S. (1992) 'Scuba diving holidays', in B. Weiler and C. M. Hall (eds) *Special Interest Tourism*, London: Belhaven.

Theobald, W. (ed.) (1994) *Global Tourism, The Next Decade*, Oxford: Butterworth Heinemann.

Turner, L. and Ash, J. (1975) *The Golden Hordes, International Tourism and the Pleasure Periphery*, London: Constable.

Um, S. and Crompton, J. L. (1987) 'Measuring residents' attachment levels in host communities', *Journal of Travel Research* Summer, 27–9.

Urry, J. (1990) *The Tourist Gaze*, London: Sage.

Wahab, S., Crampon, L. J. and Rothfield, L. M. (1976) *Tourism Marketing*, London: Tourism International Press.

Walle, A. (1993) 'Tourism and traditional people: forging equitable strategies', *Journal of Travel Research* Winter, 14–19.

Walmsley, D. and Jenkins, J. (1992) 'Cognitive distance, a neglected issue in travel research', *Journal of Travel Research* Summer, 24–9.

Wanhill, S. R. C. (1987) 'UK politics and tourism', *Tourism Management* March, 54–7.

Wanhill, S. (1992) *Tourism 2,000, A Perspective for Wales*, Cardiff: Wales Tourist Board.

West, G. (1929) *Jogging around Majorca*, Alson Rivers; republished by Black Swan, 1994.

Western Samoa Tourism Development Plan, 1992–2001 (1992) Government of

Western Samoa and Tourism Council of the South Pacific: Apia.

Westwood, M. (1989) 'Warwick Castle, safeguarding for the future through service', in Uzzell, D. *Heritage Interpretation*, London: Belhaven Press.

Wilkie, W. L. (1986) *Consumer Behavior*, New York: Wiley.

Williams, A. V. and Zelinsky, W. (1970) 'On some patterns in international tourism flows', *Economic Geography* 6, 4: 549–67.

Wind, Y. (1978) 'Issues and advances in segmentation research', *Journal of Marketing Research* August, 317–37.

Woodside, A. and Lysonski, S. (1989) 'A general model of traveler destination choice', *Journal of Travel Research*, spring, 9.

Woodside, A. G. and Sherrill, D. (1977) 'Traveler evoked and inept sets of vacation destinations', *Journal of Travel Research* 16, 1: 14–18.

WTO (World Tourist Organization) (1979) *Role and Structure of National Tourism Administrations*, Madrid: WTO.

—— (1980) *Physical Planning and Area Development for Tourism*, Madrid: WTO.

Ziffer, K. (1989) *Ecotourism, the Uneasy Alliance*, Washington: Ernst & Young.

Author index

Place index

Subject index